DIGITAL EUROPE

Seventy Questions on Rights and
Rules in the Age of AI

Carmelo Greco
Roberto Sammarchi

Parma & Sammarchi - Imprese e diritti

Copyright 2024 (November) - First edition

Parma & Sammarchi - Imprese e diritti

Casalecchio di Reno (BO)
Italy

parmasammarchi.it

CONTENTS

Title Page
Preamble — 1
Introduction — 3
1. Foreword to the reader — 5
2. Protection of personal data — 23
3. Cybersecurity — 43
4. Physical safety of workers — 64
5. Workers' rights and new technologies — 86
6. Products, machines, installations — 109
7. AI Act and new European framework — 133
Conclusions — 153
Regulations and Standards — 155
The Authors — 159

PREAMBLE

The European Union is the most highly regulated political and social context in the world. This situation arises from several factors that contribute to the creation of an extremely complex legal system, including:

a) the layering of laws, combining national and European regulations;
b) the drive to harmonize national laws by surpassing and integrating them into a coordinated vision;
c) a strong emphasis on fundamental rights and the «*(droit) acquis communautaire*» which aims to unify the visions, objectives, and obligations of Member States into a synthesis that is often challenging to achieve;
d) the original functions of regulating the common market, which focused on standards, constraints, and controls.

This book stems from a dialogue between a journalist and a lawyer who have spent many years working in the field of digital technology. It provides answers to seventy questions to help readers navigate the EU regulations shaping our technological future.
The authors share the goal of offering a concise guide for those who are not yet experts in digital technology law but, due to professional needs or personal interest, wish to embark on a journey of understanding and deeper exploration of this subject. After identifying the key regulations to examine and presenting their interconnections, all texts were used as the knowledge base for an artificial intelligence system. A structure of prompts was created to identify correlations between texts, key themes, and potential coordinated interpretations of practical issues. The entire process, followed by extensive human review and reworking, resulted in the text now presented to readers.

This book is not necessarily designed to be read from cover to cover. The unique development process has made the sections contained in the seven chapters largely independent, as each includes all the essential concepts for the topic it addresses. To achieve this, the authors opted for a certain degree of redundancy, presenting some fundamental topics (e.g., personal data regulations) organically in multiple contexts. However, the perspective and approach to the topic change each time, broadening and enriching the reader's understanding with each chapter.

This text is also dedicated to those who have never considered studying a university law manual but still wish to gain a sufficiently clear and precise understanding of European regulations on digital technology. It is with this audience in mind that the book has been created, in the hope that taking this first step will inspire further interest in the topic.

Happy reading!

The Authors

INTRODUCTION

Discussing innovation in general, and technological innovation in particular, often sparks heated debates. This shows that, despite the seemingly neutral nature of the subject, its implications for people's lives and work are so significant that they cannot be ignored. Since the dawn of the Industrial Revolution, protests like Luddism have shown that the introduction of machinery in production processes did not meet with unanimous approval, even from those who were expected to benefit from it. Fast forward from the 18th century to today, and the list of *anti-technology revolutionaries* (to borrow the title of a book by Theodore Kaczynski, better known as the Unabomber) has grown, at times intertwining with various anti-modernist movements.

Despite the opposition, it is evident that resistance to technological progress is ultimately futile. Massimo Temporelli expresses this clearly in his book *We Are Technology* (Mondadori, 2021), asserting that "our interior and exterior landscapes are technological." He invites us to imagine life "without a fork, glass, roads, heating, aqueducts, ovens, or bed springs..." Ultimately, he concludes, "we Homo sapiens need technology to survive; we cannot turn it off, exclude it, or fight it—it would be like sabotaging ourselves and our very existence."

Beyond its essential role in daily life, technology has also become indispensable in the professional sphere. This applies to the fields of both authors, a lawyer and a journalist, whose professions have been profoundly transformed by tools like word processing software and email. The latter, in particular, has evolved through innovations aimed at certifying the validity of exchanges, ensuring authenticity and traceability. Certified email and e-invoicing—digital alternatives to traditional methods—are examples of how digital rules have reshaped conventional practices.

Every innovation and technology challenges humanity as

holders of rights and responsibilities. In other words, they inevitably intersect with the vast domain of the *Ius*—the law—through a dialogue between two ever-evolving worlds: law and technological innovation. In recent years, the European Union has sought to provide a cohesive regulatory framework to address the rapid changes brought about by technological advancements. However, this remains an ongoing effort, as the pace of digital transformation often outstrips the legislative process. While significant progress has been made, much work remains.

This book aims to answer common questions that arise today, in the era of artificial intelligence, focusing on issues such as privacy, physical and digital security, workers' rights in technological contexts, and regulations governing products, machinery, and systems. Without aspiring to be exhaustive, it is designed as a concise and practical tool for anyone—entrepreneur, professional, or employee—seeking a structured overview of European laws in this domain.

Legal texts and manuals are often dense and unapproachable for those who are not legal practitioners, leading to widespread ignorance of the laws and their practical implications. For example, while everyone in Europe is talking about the European Artificial Intelligence Regulation, very few people—fortunately for this book's relevance—have read all 144 pages of it.

Readers who follow along will find clear explanations of the key topics and issues in digital technology law. The text is designed to be accessible and engaging, offering examples and a straightforward style that makes even complex legal topics comprehensible. The goal is to provide useful insights to navigate regulations, case studies, and future trends while addressing the ethical and practical challenges of this rapidly evolving field.

1. FOREWORD TO THE READER

Who is this book for?

This book targets a broad audience, including professionals, businesses, technology and legal practitioners, as well as anyone interested in better understanding the dynamics of innovation and artificial intelligence (AI). The continuous evolution of technologies and the expansion of AI into our daily lives have made a more informed and mindful approach to these topics essential, both for developers and users. This volume aims to address the needs of those interacting with technological innovation in various capacities, helping them understand the opportunities and risks associated with the use of AI and emerging technologies.

The text provides guidance for decision-makers like entrepreneurs and managers, as well as for legal or technical consultants who need to navigate the complex and ever-changing regulations governing the use of advanced technologies. For instance, entrepreneurs will find a guide on how to adopt AI tools in compliance with European and national laws, starting with Regulation (EU) 2024/1689, which sets harmonized rules for AI development and usage within the European Union. While AI represents a significant competitive advantage for businesses, the risks can be high without a proper understanding of the associated rules and responsibilities—particularly regarding legal compliance, data protection, and privacy safeguards.

Legal consultants will also find this book a valuable tool for deepening their understanding of the legal implications of innovation. Since the introduction of regulations such as the General Data Protection Regulation (GDPR), data protection has become a central issue in every sector. Moreover, the use of AI introduces new challenges and complexities. Professionals must be able to interpret and apply these regulations correctly to support their clients effectively, designing compliance procedures tailored to the new technological context.

Developers and engineers can also benefit from this book. While AI primarily pertains to the technical domain, its development and use cannot ignore the regulations governing its deployment. AI system developers, for instance, must understand the ethical and legal principles underlying the responsible use of these technologies to ensure their products not only comply with the law but also promote a human-centered vision of AI—the only sustainable approach.

Finally, even those without technical expertise but who wish to gain a clear and accessible perspective on how technological innovation and AI are impacting society can benefit from this book. Whether you are a professional seeking practical guidelines or a curious reader exploring how technology shapes our lives, this book provides useful tools to understand and navigate the technological future in an informed and responsible manner.

Why should I read this book?

The technological revolution we are experiencing profoundly affects many aspects of our lives—from business to social relationships and individual experiences. AI, in particular, is radically transforming how we work, communicate, and make decisions, raising critical ethical, legal, and social questions.

One of the main reasons to read this book is to understand how emerging technologies, especially AI, are influencing the regulatory landscape on both a European and global scale. The European Union has introduced a set of rules aimed at ensuring the ethical and responsible development of AI technologies, striving to create a common legal framework that protects fundamental human rights, such as privacy, security, and non-discrimination. Understanding these regulations is essential not only for those working in the tech sector but also for anyone using advanced technologies in their daily lives.

The book also addresses the needs of those grappling with the rapid evolution of technologies and wondering how to use them safely and effectively. While it is not a technical or legal manual, it offers a comprehensive perspective on how AI can be integrated into daily life and business operations. In a world where intelligent technologies are increasingly prevalent—from smart homes to virtual assistants and personalized online services—it is crucial to understand both the potential and the risks associated with these innovations.

Issues related to AI, data protection, and cybersecurity are often seen as highly technical and difficult to grasp. However, this volume seeks to tackle these topics in a clear and understandable way, even for those without a technical background. It allows readers to acquire the necessary knowledge to understand the ongoing dynamics and make informed decisions in the context of an increasingly digitized future.

Yes, innovation and technology are important, but there's more to life...

This question reflects a common sentiment about the growing ubiquity of technology in our lives. While innovation and technology play a central role in modern life, they should not overshadow other aspects of our existence, such as human relationships, culture, or the overall quality of life.

That said, technological innovation has undoubtedly brought immense benefits. Advances in medicine, for example, have led to more accurate diagnoses and effective treatments. Work has become more flexible and accessible through digital platforms and remote working. Education has been enriched with digital resources, enabling personalized and remote learning. Even in our daily lives, technology has simplified routine tasks, saved us time, and allowed us to connect with people worldwide.

Despite these advantages, it is fair to ask whether our lives are becoming overly dependent on innovation and how our well-being is affected. This underscores the importance of designing technologies not just to solve operational problems but also to enhance people's quality of life without compromising fundamental values like freedom and human dignity.

Moreover, if innovation is not carefully managed, it risks alienating us from what makes us truly human. Relationships, creativity, empathy, and direct experience are dimensions that technology can facilitate but never replace. For instance, while social networks have revolutionized communication, they have also raised concerns about the authenticity of interactions and the risk of social isolation. Similarly, digital work has increased flexibility but may lead to a blurring of boundaries between professional and personal life, potentially impacting psychological well-being.

Considering the importance that workplaces have assumed over time as places of social interaction and rights protection, it's easy to understand that remote work—where employees operate most of the time as isolated individuals—brings profound changes to union organizations, contractual methods, career prospects, welfare solutions, ergonomics, and the balance between work and family life.

Regarding this last aspect, legal professionals have certainly noticed numerous cohabitation crises that emerged during the pandemic period. During this time, the blurring of spaces and schedules between work and home environments caused conflicts to erupt, in some cases even revealing genuine psychiatric conditions involving both adults and young people deprived of normal contact with school settings and peers.

The risk of alienation is particularly significant in the context of artificial intelligence. Massive use of AI to perform increasingly complex tasks and automated decisions can lead to a loss of control by individuals. Not coincidentally, the European regulation on artificial intelligence emphasizes the need to ensure that human beings always remain at the center of the decision-making process, guaranteeing that AI is used transparently and that there is always the possibility of human intervention when necessary.

Innovation should free up our time and energy so we can dedicate ourselves more to activities that align with our well-being and interests. For this reason, the true success of innovation should lie in its ability to improve the quality of our lives without replacing the fundamental aspects that make us who we are.

Yesterday it was the internet and social media; today it's artificial intelligence. What's next?

There is widespread concern about the speed at which technology is developing and uncertainty about its long-term consequences. If yesterday the internet and social networks represented a revolution that transformed how we communicate, interact, and work, today artificial intelligence presents itself as the new frontier of technological change, promising an impact as deep, if not deeper, on every aspect of our lives.

To answer this question, we must consider not only where we are today but also how technological innovation has developed over recent decades and what emerging trends are shaping the future. The introduction of the internet opened the doors to an interconnected, globalized world where information is accessible to an ever-growing number of people at increasingly rapid speeds. Social networks accelerated this dynamic, offering platforms where it's possible not only to access information but also to express oneself and build virtual communities. However, the flip side of this rapid evolution has been the emergence of issues related to privacy, disinformation, manipulation of information, and even the compulsive use of new tools.

With the advent of artificial intelligence, we are facing an even more pervasive transformation. AI is already changing the way we work, live, and make decisions, automating processes that until a few years ago required human intervention. From medical diagnosis to autonomous driving, from energy resource management to industrial production, AI has the potential to make many activities more efficient and precise. However, this evolution raises questions about the impact these technologies will have on employment, ethics, and data security. The European regulation on artificial intelligence, in this sense, seeks to provide a normative response to these challenges, imposing clear rules to ensure that AI is developed and used safely and responsibly.

But where will this evolution take us? One possibility is that artificial intelligence becomes increasingly integrated into our daily lives, to the point of becoming almost invisible. AI systems could manage much of the infrastructure and services we use—from healthcare to transportation, from public administration to entertainment—allowing us to live in an increasingly automated and interconnected world. However, such a scenario requires deep reflection on how we want these technologies to be used. We cannot allow technological innovation to escape human control or become a threat to people's fundamental rights.

The ethical and social challenges connected to artificial intelligence are numerous. A central aspect is the issue of work. While automation and AI can improve production efficiency, they also risk replacing many functions currently performed by humans, with potentially dramatic consequences for employment. This phenomenon, known as "technological unemployment," is already underway in various sectors and requires a response at the level of public policies. Training and professional retraining are therefore fundamental to ensure that workers can adapt to new work contexts and perform new roles made possible by the reorganization of production processes.

Another relevant aspect concerns privacy and the management of personal data. Artificial intelligence is based on the analysis of enormous quantities of data, often collected from users themselves through digital devices and online platforms. The protection of privacy thus becomes an absolute priority, and regulators must ensure that data is handled ethically and in compliance with data protection laws. In this context, the regulation on AI aims to establish clear limits on the use of artificial intelligence systems that could compromise people's rights, such as those used for facial recognition or automated profiling.

Finally, another element we cannot overlook is the social impact of artificial intelligence. While these technologies promise to improve the quality of life in many ways, there is a risk they could exacerbate existing inequalities. Large tech companies, which have the resources necessary to develop and implement advanced AI systems, could acquire even greater economic and social power, leaving behind small businesses and less developed nations. The digital divide could thus widen further, creating new forms of social exclusion.

Artificial intelligence is leading us toward a future increasingly dominated by technology, but how we manage this transition will depend on the choices we make today. If we can integrate technological innovation with a strong sense of ethical and social responsibility, we can make the most of the opportunities offered by AI while minimizing the risks. Where we will end up depends on us: the future of technology is in our hands, and it is essential that it remains at the service of humanity—not the other way around.

To be in the clear, all I need is to do what my consultant tells me to do.

Relying on a competent and well-prepared consultant is certainly a wise choice, especially in a complex and constantly evolving context like technological innovation and regulatory compliance. However, merely following what the consultant says without fully understanding the implications of your choices or the applicable regulations may not be sufficient. Consulting is a valuable tool for navigating rules and obligations, but it cannot replace an informed understanding by the organization or the individual concerned.

Let's start from the premise that regulations—especially those related to innovation and technology—are constantly being updated. The field of artificial intelligence is an example of how laws can change rapidly to keep pace with technological advances. For instance, Regulation (EU) 2024/1689 on Artificial Intelligence, one of the most recent and comprehensive laws on AI, has introduced a series of obligations and limitations that were unpredictable until now. The regulation requires those who develop, sell, or use AI systems to comply with a set of requirements, including risk assessment, transparency, data governance, and traceability of operations. The importance of a consultant, in this context, lies in the support they can offer to interpret and apply the new rules, but they cannot eliminate the individual or corporate responsibility to stay updated, fully understand the regulations, and apply them concretely.

Relying solely on a consultant's opinion without making an effort to understand at least the basic principles of the relevant regulations can lead to two main risks. The first is that, although the consultant may provide correct guidance, the legal responsibility remains with the company or individual acting. If violations or non-compliance occur, it will not be the consultant who is legally accountable but those who decided whether or not to implement the provided recommendations. This is particularly true in the field of data protection and artificial intelligence, where penalties for non-compliance with regulations, such as the European General Data Protection Regulation (GDPR), can be very severe.

The second risk is that regulations can be interpreted differently depending on the specific context of the organization. A consultant can provide guidance based on their own experience and current regulations but may not have a complete view of the internal dynamics and processes of the company or entity they assist. If the recipient of the consultancy lacks sufficient understanding of the issues addressed, they might accept solutions that, in the long term, are not suitable for their needs or do not consider operational peculiarities. Even if the consultant is highly competent, only those deeply involved in the management and daily activities of the organization can fully assess whether the proposed solutions are appropriate and sustainable.

It is important to adopt a proactive approach. Passively following a consultant's recommendations without actively participating in the decision-making process can leave you unprepared for changes. Regulations in the field of technology —such as those concerning artificial intelligence, cybersecurity, and data protection—are constantly evolving to keep pace with technological innovations and new risks. A company or professional who does not invest in keeping their knowledge updated on these topics risks encountering difficulties when new requirements or regulations emerge.

Having a basic understanding and an active interest in regulatory dynamics allows for anticipating potential problems and adopting more effective solutions whose compliance endures over time.

It's impossible to keep up with all the National laws and regulations, let alone the European ones.

This statement, although understandable, reflects a perception that doesn't entirely match reality. It's true that the complexity of laws and regulations, especially in the field of technology and innovation, can seem overwhelming. However, there are tools and strategies that allow us to tackle this task effectively without being overwhelmed by the sheer volume of measures on the subject.

First of all, it's important to consider that the National and European regulatory systems have made significant progress in attempting to simplify and harmonize regulations, especially in highly innovative areas like artificial intelligence, data protection, and cybersecurity. At the European level, the adoption of regulations like the General Data Protection Regulation (GDPR) and the recent Regulation (EU) 2024/1689 on Artificial Intelligence have created a clearer and more uniform regulatory framework for all Member States. The main advantage of European regulations is that, once published and within the indicated timelines, they become immediately applicable in all Union countries, reducing the need to deal with fragmented and often conflicting national regulations. This principle of harmonization reduces complexity for companies and professionals operating in multiple Member States, as they have to comply with a single common regulation instead of a patchwork of national laws.

At the national level, there are also many resources that allow one to stay updated on regulations. Companies and consultants operating in regulated sectors can rely on digital tools and databases that, in real time, provide access to relevant laws and decisions; artificial intelligence itself, increasingly integrated into research tools, offers opportunities to speed up and make efficient the process of identifying obligations to apply in specific cases. Moreover, regulations are often accompanied by guidelines provided by the authorities responsible for their enforcement, such as the Data Protection Authority or the European Commission—guidelines that offer significant assistance during the application phase.

Moreover, in such a complex and constantly evolving world, no organization can realistically know in advance the details of every rule that governs its activity. Hence the importance of strategic management of regulatory compliance. In other words, it's possible to adopt a systematic approach that allows one to identify the most relevant regulations for one's sector and manage them efficiently. For businesses, this can mean creating an internal team dedicated to compliance or entrusting specialized consultants, with the goal of constantly monitoring regulatory developments and ensuring that the organization remains compliant with applicable laws.

Technology offers valuable solutions to tackle this challenge. Compliance management software allows the automation of much of the work related to regulatory monitoring and updating business practices based on new laws. Digital tools can quickly and accurately analyze new regulations and provide suggestions on how to adapt business processes to ensure compliance. This approach significantly reduces manual workload and helps avoid penalties due to non-compliance.

Nevertheless, it remains a fact that keeping up with all regulations can seem extremely arduous. However, it's helpful to remember that regulations don't have the same relevance for all obligated parties. A small business that doesn't handle sensitive data, for example, may have fewer obligations compared to a multinational that processes large volumes of personal information in a cross-border context. Similarly, regulations related to artificial intelligence are particularly pertinent for those who develop or use AI systems but are not necessarily a priority for other businesses that operate in more traditional ways. One of the first steps to manage this complexity is to precisely identify which laws and regulations actually concern one's field of activity.

An important aspect is also the support offered by trade associations, professional orders, and Chambers of Commerce. These entities often provide regulatory update services and organize seminars and training courses for their members, helping them stay informed about legislative news relevant to their sector. Participating in such initiatives can be a fundamental resource for anyone wishing to stay updated without being overwhelmed by the informational load.

What do I risk if I underestimate these laws and regulations?

Underestimating laws and regulations, particularly in the technology and innovation sectors, can expose businesses to significant risks on legal, financial, and reputational levels. Regulations are not designed to complicate business activities or individual efforts; they aim to ensure the ethical and legal development and use of technologies. Ignoring or minimizing their importance can have severe consequences.

From a legal standpoint, the risk is clear. Many European and national regulations in AI and data protection come with strict penalties for non-compliance. For instance, violations of the GDPR can lead to substantial fines, potentially calculated as a percentage of the organization's global annual turnover. Similarly, the AI Regulation (EU) 2024/1689 includes penalties for failing to meet transparency, safety, and traceability requirements, especially for high-risk AI systems. Non-compliance may force a business to stop using specific systems or withdraw them from the market, resulting in operational and financial setbacks.

Reputational risk is another significant concern. Trust from customers, business partners, and the public is invaluable and can be difficult to regain once lost. A company sanctioned for non-compliance—especially in sensitive areas such as data protection and AI—risks severe reputational damage. Modern consumers are increasingly vigilant about how their data is handled and the transparency of the companies they engage with. A single violation can undermine public trust, resulting in lost customers and contracts, and cause lasting reputational harm that is hard to repair. In today's competitive market, where trust is often a key deciding factor for consumers, reputational damage can outweigh financial penalties.

Non-compliance with regulations can also lead to the inability to use tools or technologies legally, which may severely limit a company's competitiveness. European regulations are not only designed to protect citizens' rights but also to create a safer and more uniform market where businesses can operate. Ignoring these rules means failing to fully exploit the opportunities offered by digitalization and innovation.

Another significant risk is civil liability. If a non-compliant technology causes harm—be it material or moral—to a customer or user, the company could face lawsuits in civil court, in addition to potential criminal liability. This could result in substantial financial damages. For example, consider cases involving artificial intelligence used in critical sectors like healthcare or transportation. If a non-compliant system causes an accident or malfunction, the organization will be liable for damages, not only financially but also in terms of responsibility for the health and safety of the people affected.

Finally, organizations that invest in compliance often gain additional benefits beyond avoiding penalties. A focus on regulatory compliance can lead to improved internal processes, enhanced data security, and better service quality for customers. Adapting to regulations can also foster greater operational efficiency, reduce the risk of cyberattacks, and enhance transparency in the marketplace. These advantages provide a competitive edge over organizations that neglect or underestimate the importance of compliance.

Who guarantees that, after making my organization compliant with the law, new regulations won't come up and force me to start over?

This concern is quite common among businesses and professionals operating in highly regulated sectors such as technology and innovation. It is true that the regulatory landscape evolves rapidly, but it is equally true that the legal framework we operate within, at both the national and European levels, is designed to ensure stability and certainty. While this does not exclude updates to adapt to technological advances and emerging risks, the law is not intended to destabilize businesses.

No one can guarantee that new regulations will not be introduced or that laws will not be updated. However, one of the primary functions of the legal system is to provide predictability and legal certainty. For example, new regulations like the European Union Artificial Intelligence Regulation (EU) 2024/1689 are not designed to impose abrupt changes without allowing businesses sufficient time to adapt. The European regulatory process typically includes transition periods and extensive consultations with stakeholders before implementing new rules, ensuring companies are neither caught off guard nor forced to overhaul their systems from scratch.

Many recent regulations are drafted to be flexible enough to accommodate rapid technological evolution. For instance, the General Data Protection Regulation (GDPR), one of the strictest regulatory frameworks, was written to remain applicable even with the introduction of new technologies. Despite its enactment in 2018, the GDPR remains fully relevant in the context of artificial intelligence and other emerging innovations. This demonstrates that European regulations are designed to address current challenges while anticipating future ones.

If an organization has implemented a robust and dynamic compliance management system, adapting to new regulatory changes does not necessarily mean starting from scratch. A good compliance system is not rigid; it is designed for adaptability. Companies that invest in solid compliance frameworks—including continuous monitoring of regulations and fostering a compliance-oriented corporate culture—find it much easier to adjust to regulatory changes. This approach makes compliance part of the organization's operational management, rather than a disruptive event requiring drastic interventions.

Not all regulations—it's worth noting—have an immediate or direct impact on organizations. Often, regulations differentiate between sectors and types of technology, imposing varying obligations depending on the complexity and risk level associated with specific tools. For example, a small business that uses AI systems in a limited capacity and not in high-risk contexts will not face the same requirements as a large company developing advanced AI technologies for critical applications. Regulations are typically calibrated to account for specific contexts, minimizing the risk of having to "start over" every time a new rule is introduced.

That said, maintaining compliance requires organizations to adopt a proactive attitude and prepare for change. One effective approach is to continuously monitor regulatory developments and actively participate in public consultation processes, which often precede the adoption of new laws. Many organizations find it useful to maintain close relationships with trade associations, professional bodies, and legal advisors who can provide timely updates and advice on how to handle potential regulatory changes.

Does reading this book mean I won't need to consult specialists?

While this book provides an in-depth and detailed overview of complex topics like innovation, artificial intelligence, and related regulations, it cannot replace the role of a specialist. The book is undoubtedly a useful tool for gaining foundational knowledge of the legal and technological issues surrounding innovation, but specialized consultancy remains essential in many contexts, especially when specific situations require the assumption of direct responsibility.

There are two main reasons why reading a text, no matter how detailed and useful, cannot substitute for expert advice. The first is the complexity and variability of regulations. The book can provide an accurate description of the laws and regulations currently in force, but their practical application can vary greatly depending on the specific context of the organization or individual reading it. Regulations, particularly those related to artificial intelligence and data protection, are complex and subject to interpretations that can differ based on specific circumstances. For example, the frequently mentioned Artificial Intelligence Regulation (EU) 2024/1689 sets forth a range of obligations that vary considerably depending on the type of AI system being used, the sector in which the organization operates, and the level of risk associated with deploying such technologies. Only an expert can accurately assess these factors and provide tailored advice on how to meet legal requirements.

Moreover, the rapid pace of technological evolution necessitates continuous updates, which often require specialized consultation. Emerging technologies like artificial intelligence, blockchain, or the Internet of Things (IoT) are constantly evolving, as are the regulations governing them. While this book offers a solid foundation, regulations can change quickly and require ongoing updates. Specialists, such as technology law experts or consultants, are tasked with monitoring these developments and offering specific guidance applicable to individual cases. Therefore, while the book can help you understand the general framework, it is unlikely to provide exhaustive answers to complex situations or specific questions that may arise when implementing new technologies.

The second reason to seek expert advice is the need for tailored solutions. Every company, organization, or individual has unique needs when it comes to technology, innovation, and regulatory compliance. What works for a large corporation may not be suitable for a small business or a sole professional. A book cannot account for the specificities of each situation, whereas a consultant can analyze the unique needs of the organization and provide customized solutions. For example, a startup developing AI systems for healthcare will have very different regulatory requirements than a company using AI to optimize logistics. Even if the book provides valuable insights, only an expert can ensure that the information is applied correctly and aligns with the specific needs of the operating context. Additionally, in some cases, the law itself mandates the involvement of a specialist, as seen in the GDPR's requirement for certain organizations to appoint a Data Protection Officer (DPO).

But I think common sense is enough...

The idea that common sense might be sufficient to tackle the challenges posed by technological innovation and associated regulations can seem appealing. However, the current legal and technological context is so complex and constantly evolving that relying solely on common sense risks being not only insufficient but even dangerous. Common sense, understood as a natural ability to make rational and prudent decisions, can certainly be useful in many everyday situations. But when it comes to technical regulations and complex laws, something more is needed: in-depth knowledge and awareness of the legal framework in which one operates. Especially since regulations are not simply guidelines based on general principles but constitute a set of detailed rules that must be rigorously followed. An evident example is the protection of personal data: the European General Data Protection Regulation (GDPR) imposes stringent rules on how data must be collected, processed, stored, and protected. It's not enough to act cautiously or with the best intentions; it's necessary to know and correctly apply the current regulations to avoid legal violations.

Moreover, the concept of "common sense" varies from person to person. What may seem sensible to one individual in a certain context might not be for another (and even less might coincide with what is stipulated by law). Regulations, particularly those related to technology, have been developed precisely to provide clear and uniform rules that go beyond individual perceptions. This is especially important in sectors like artificial intelligence, where risks of discrimination, privacy violations, or misuse of data can have very serious consequences. The AI regulation, for example, establishes specific requirements for high-risk artificial intelligence systems, such as those used for evaluating candidates in recruitment or monitoring workers. The requirements include transparency, traceability, data governance, and continuous monitoring of the system's performance. Acting based solely on common sense, without following specific obligations, can lead to unintentional but equally sanctionable violations.

Many modern regulations have been introduced precisely to mitigate risks associated with using technologies in ways that might escape simple common sense. The regulation on artificial intelligence, for instance, was conceived to address complex problems like algorithmic transparency and the ethical and social impact of automated decisions. In many cases, these problems are so intricate that they require not only regulatory compliance but also a scientifically planned approach to be resolved. Transparency, to cite one of the aspects mentioned earlier, doesn't just mean explaining how an AI system works but also implies that the results produced are verifiable and that the data used are managed securely and in compliance with regulations. It's difficult to tackle such complex issues without adequate preparation and expert support.

The merits of common sense in the daily life of organizations should not be underestimated, but it must be combined with a rigorous approach to understanding and implementing regulations, which often requires the support of experts with specific competencies.

2. PROTECTION OF PERSONAL DATA

How can artificial intelligence technologies improve personal data protection?

Artificial intelligence (AI) technologies offer tremendous potential for enhancing personal data protection, particularly in a world where the volume of data being processed is growing exponentially and cybersecurity threats are becoming increasingly sophisticated. AI can be applied across various areas to make data protection systems more efficient, adaptive, and secure, ensuring more accurate and timely management of sensitive information.

One of the main advantages of AI in the field of personal data protection is its ability to identify threats and vulnerabilities in real time. AI-based systems can analyze massive amounts of data much faster and more efficiently than traditional systems, detecting anomalies and suspicious behavior that could indicate a security breach. For example, machine learning technologies can monitor network traffic and identify unauthorized access attempts or patterns that suggest an ongoing cyberattack. This type of analysis allows for prompt action to mitigate risks, reducing exposure time to threats and limiting potential negative impacts on individuals and organizations.

AI also contributes to improving personal data protection through advanced access management. AI systems can implement dynamic access controls based on various factors, such as user identity, context, and behavior. These systems analyze user activities in real time and compare them with standard behavior models. If anomalies are detected—such as attempts to access sensitive data by an employee without proper authorization—AI can immediately block the action and alert security personnel. This dynamic approach to authorization and authentication represents a significant improvement over traditional static rule-based access systems.

Another way AI enhances personal data protection is through advanced encryption and automated cryptographic key management. AI systems can automatically generate, distribute, and manage encryption keys used to protect data performed on encrypted data without needing to decrypt it, thus protecting sensitive information even during processing.

AI further improves personal data protection by enabling more effective log management. AI-powered systems can rapidly analyze and correlate user and application activity logs, identifying potential violations or anomalies. This capability is particularly useful in complex environments where traditional log management is slow and inefficient. Automated and continuous analysis allows for real-time detection of unauthorized access attempts or data manipulation, improving overall security.

Moreover, AI can facilitate compliance with data protection regulations, such as the European General Data Protection Regulation (GDPR). Advanced AI systems can monitor business processes and continuously verify compliance with legal requirements, immediately flagging any violations or gaps in security protocols. For instance, an AI system could automatically ensure that personal data is processed in accordance with principles such as data minimization and purpose limitation, flagging any non-compliant activities. This automation not only enhances data protection but also reduces the workload associated with regulatory compliance management.

Another area where AI has a positive impact is in preventing privacy breaches through advanced anonymization and pseudonymization techniques. AI can develop algorithms that more effectively anonymize data, reducing the risk of personal information being traced back to individuals. Similarly, AI can help ensure consistency in anonymization processes, even when combining different datasets, thereby protecting user privacy in scenarios involving large-scale data processing.

However, it is important to note that while AI offers powerful tools for improving personal data protection, it also presents challenges, particularly regarding algorithm transparency and explainability. The non-deterministic nature of certain AI processes can make it difficult to explain "why" a system has reached a specific result—results that are often "probably" correct but not logically deducible, as required in traditional legal approaches.

This is why the use of AI in data protection must be carefully regulated to ensure that personal rights are respected and that decisions made by automated systems are as transparent and understandable as possible, minimizing the risk of violations.

How do European regulations ensure the security of personal data in electronic communications?

European regulations, particularly the General Data Protection Regulation (GDPR) and the ePrivacy Regulation, prioritize the security of personal data in electronic communications. These regulations address challenges arising from the increasingly pervasive use of digital technologies and the global interconnectedness of networks, aiming to balance innovation, privacy protection, and data security. Both frameworks emphasize the protection of fundamental rights and impose stringent obligations on companies and organizations that process personal data in their daily activities, including those involving electronic communications.

The GDPR serves as the overarching framework for personal data protection in Europe, introducing strict rules requiring entities that collect, use, or store data to implement appropriate measures to ensure its security. In the context of electronic communications, companies such as email service providers, messaging platforms, social networks, and telecommunications operators must ensure that user data is protected throughout its lifecycle. This includes implementing encryption techniques to safeguard information exchanged between users and platforms, ensuring that data is not shared with third parties without consent, and promptly notifying authorities and affected users in the event of a breach.

One significant contribution of the GDPR to the security of electronic communications is the introduction of privacy "by design" and "by default" principles. These principles mandate that data protection be integrated into the initial design of systems or services ("by design") and that default settings guarantee the highest level of protection possible ("by default"). For example, messaging applications must automatically encrypt communications, and user data should not be collected or retained beyond what is necessary. Such measures reduce the risk of unauthorized data exposure and enhance user trust in electronic communication platforms.

In addition to the GDPR, the forthcoming ePrivacy Regulation focuses specifically on protecting privacy in electronic communications. This regulation aims to strengthen rules on the confidentiality of digital communications, ensuring that email conversations, messages, and other forms of electronic communication are handled confidentially. A key provision of ePrivacy is reinforcing consent as the legal basis for processing data in electronic communications. Users must be clearly informed and must give explicit consent for data processing, such as tracking activity through cookies.

The ePrivacy Regulation also seeks to strengthen protections against spam and unsolicited communications by tightening rules on electronic direct marketing. Under these new provisions, companies will face stricter requirements to prevent promotional communications via email or SMS without explicit user consent. This not only enhances privacy protection but also reduces the risk of electronic communications being exploited for illegal activities like phishing or other cybercrimes.

Another critical aspect involves safeguarding data during transfers outside the European Union. The GDPR stipulates that personal data may only be transferred to third countries if they ensure an adequate level of protection as determined by the EU. For electronic communications, this means that service providers operating in non-EU countries must demonstrate compliance with security standards equivalent to those in Europe. The now-invalidated Privacy Shield agreement between the EU and the United States previously governed such transfers, but companies must now rely on standard contractual clauses or other legal mechanisms outlined in the GDPR to ensure data security during international transfers.

Lastly, European regulations mandate the adoption of technical and organizational measures to prevent data breaches. The GDPR requires companies to implement protections such as encryption, pseudonymization, and other advanced techniques to ensure the confidentiality, integrity, and availability of personal data. In the event of a breach, the regulation establishes a notification system that obliges companies to promptly inform both supervisory authorities and affected users, minimizing the risk of further damage.

What are the implications of the European General Data Protection Regulation (GDPR) for the use of personal data in cloud computing services?

The GDPR has had a significant impact on the use of personal data in cloud computing services. The cloud represents a critical technology for managing, processing, and storing large volumes of data across remote infrastructures, often located in different jurisdictions. This approach offers numerous advantages, including scalability, cost efficiency, and ease of data access from anywhere. However, the GDPR imposes strict rules on personal data processing within these services, prioritizing privacy and information security.

One of the primary implications involves the responsibility of the data controller. The GDPR distinguishes between the data controller— the entity that determines the purposes and means of personal data processing—and the data processor, which may be a cloud service provider. In this context, the data controller must ensure that the data processor (the cloud provider) complies with all the rules set out in the regulation. This means that companies or organizations using cloud services must verify that their providers implement adequate security measures to protect personal data and handle it in accordance with the regulation.

A critical component of this responsibility involves formal contractual agreements between the data controller and the processor. The GDPR requires a formal contract to be established between the company using cloud services and the service provider. The contract must include specific provisions ensuring data protection, such as requiring the provider to implement appropriate technical and organizational measures to secure personal data, restrict access to authorized personnel, and ensure transparency about data processing activities. Additionally, the contract must stipulate that the cloud provider cannot transfer data to third parties without the controller's consent and that, in cases of subcontracting, the cloud provider remains responsible for the actions of its subcontractors.

Another central implication of the GDPR concerns data localization and international transfers outside the European Union. Many cloud services operate on globally distributed infrastructures, making it unclear where data is physically stored or processed. The GDPR states that personal data may be transferred outside the EU only if the destination country provides an adequate level of protection as recognized by the European Commission or if the transfer is covered by appropriate safeguards, such as standard contractual clauses or binding corporate rules. Therefore, companies using cloud computing services must ensure their providers comply with these rules and adopt appropriate measures to protect data during international transfers.

The GDPR also mandates the protection of data subjects' rights.

When personal data is stored or processed on cloud platforms, individuals retain the right to access, correct, delete, or restrict the processing of their data. Companies using cloud services must ensure that their providers can uphold these rights, offering tools to ensure individuals can exercise their rights promptly. For example, if a customer requests data deletion (the right to be forgotten), the cloud service provider must fulfill this request within a reasonable timeframe and ensure that data is completely removed from all copies and backups. This can be particularly challenging in cloud environments, where data may be replicated across multiple servers and geographic regions.

Furthermore, the GDPR requires companies to implement appropriate security measures to protect personal data stored in the cloud. These measures include using encryption techniques during data transfer and storage. Encrypting data in the cloud is critical to ensure that, even in the event of unauthorized access to a provider's servers, personal data remains secure. Additional security measures include secure credential management, activity monitoring, and the ability to detect and respond swiftly to potential security breaches.

Finally, one of the most significant implications of the GDPR is the obligation to report personal data breaches. If a breach occurs, companies using cloud services must notify the competent supervisory authority within 72 hours of becoming aware of the incident. In the cloud computing context, this means cloud providers must be capable of quickly detecting any security breaches and promptly informing their customers so they can fulfill their notification obligations. This requires close collaboration between cloud service providers and their clients to ensure timely and transparent communication in the event of security incidents.

How can technological innovation and privacy protection be balanced?

Balancing technological innovation with privacy protection is one of the most complex challenges of our time, particularly in an era where personal data has become essential for operating many advanced technologies, including artificial intelligence (AI), machine learning, and the Internet of Things (IoT). On the one hand, innovation requires access to large volumes of data to improve decision-making processes, optimize system performance, and personalize services. On the other hand, privacy protection is a fundamental right that must be safeguarded, especially when sensitive information about individuals' private lives is involved.

Key methods for balancing innovation and privacy include pseudonymization and anonymization of data. Pseudonymization transforms personal data so that it can no longer be directly associated with an individual without additional information, which must be stored separately. Anonymization, in contrast, ensures that data can no longer be traced back to an identifiable individual. These techniques are particularly useful in contexts requiring large-scale data processing for research, analysis, or technology development, as they reduce privacy risks while preserving the ability to derive value from the data.

Transparency also plays a central role in balancing innovation and privacy protection. Companies and organizations that process personal data must be clear with users about which data is collected, how it will be used, who will have access to it, and how long it will be retained. Informed consent is a fundamental element of the GDPR, and individuals must be enabled to freely and knowingly provide their consent, particularly for advanced technologies that could impact their privacy. Ensuring adequate transparency not only protects individuals' rights but also builds trust in new technologies, facilitating the adoption and use of innovative services.

Encryption and other advanced security techniques represent another step toward balancing innovation and privacy. Encryption is an essential tool for protecting personal data during transmission and storage. Even when data is used for innovative purposes—such as AI algorithm development or predictive analytics—encryption ensures that only authorized individuals can access sensitive information. Technologies like blockchain can further enhance transparency and security in data processing by providing a verifiable trail of all transactions and processes related to personal data.

Data Protection Impact Assessments (DPIAs) are another tool under the GDPR that helps companies identify and mitigate privacy risks arising from new technologies. Before launching an innovative project involving personal data processing, conducting a DPIA is a best practice to understand potential risks and implement appropriate measures to minimize them. This approach prevents privacy issues and ensures that technological innovation proceeds in compliance with current regulations.

Finally, promoting a culture of accountability is essential. Organizations must invest in employee training to ensure everyone understands the importance of data protection and is aware of the regulations and best practices to follow. This way, technological innovation will not be perceived as a threat to privacy but as an opportunity to develop solutions that respect individuals' fundamental rights.

How can blockchain technology be used to protect personal data?

Blockchain technology offers numerous opportunities to enhance personal data protection due to its intrinsic features of transparency, security, and immutability. Although blockchain was originally developed to support cryptocurrencies like Bitcoin, its applications have expanded to many other fields, including personal data protection. Blockchain's unique attributes, such as decentralization and the integrity of recorded information, make it particularly suitable for addressing critical challenges associated with data protection in the digital age.

In a blockchain, data is not stored on a single server or managed by a single entity but distributed across a network of "nodes" that validate and record transactions. This means no single entity has complete control over the data, reducing the risk of security breaches from unauthorized access or centralized cyberattacks. This decentralization significantly enhances data protection by eliminating single points of failure that malicious actors could exploit.

Another key advantage of blockchain is its immutability. Once information is recorded on a blockchain, it cannot be altered or deleted unless a rigorous process involving the entire network is followed. This ensures the integrity of personal data, as any attempts to alter or manipulate the information would be easily detectable. This feature is especially relevant for protecting sensitive data, as it allows for an audit trail of all modifications and ensures data remains intact and protected from unauthorized tampering.

Blockchain can also improve the secure and transparent management of user consent. Under regulations like the GDPR, explicit consent is a fundamental requirement for processing personal data. Using blockchain, user decisions regarding the use of their data can be immutably recorded, ensuring that consent preferences are always respected and traceable. This mechanism provides greater transparency for both users and organizations, as any changes to data permissions can be verified on a public or private blockchain, reducing the risk of disputes or misunderstandings.

Another notable application of blockchain in personal data protection is pseudonymization. While blockchain was not natively designed to protect user privacy, pseudonymization techniques can be implemented to replace personal data with unique identifiers that do not directly reveal individuals' identities. This enables transactions to be recorded on a blockchain without exposing sensitive data, ensuring that personal information remains protected even when the blockchain is publicly accessible. This technique is particularly useful for sharing or transferring data among different actors or services, maintaining a high level of security and confidentiality.

Blockchain can also enhance access control management for personal data. Using smart contracts—self-executing programs recorded on a blockchain—access to personal data can be automated and monitored securely. For instance, a company could use smart contracts to allow access to data only to individuals or entities meeting specific criteria or having the appropriate consent. This ensures that access to personal data occurs strictly according to user-defined rules and preferences, reducing the risk of unauthorized access or misuse.

Furthermore, blockchain provides greater transparency in personal data processing, allowing users to verify exactly how and when their data is used. Thanks to blockchain's distributed and immutable nature, every operation involving personal data can be verifiably recorded, creating a transparent ledger of data-related activities. This is particularly useful for ensuring compliance with data protection regulations, such as the GDPR, and building user trust in service providers handling their data.

What are the challenges of advanced encryption in protecting personal data?

Advanced encryption is a critical tool for protecting personal data, serving as a barrier against unauthorized access and ensuring that only legitimate users can decrypt sensitive information. However, implementing advanced encryption presents challenges that can impact its effectiveness in protecting personal data. These challenges include key management, system performance, regulatory compliance, and balancing security with accessibility.

Keys are fundamental to the encryption process, as they are required for both encrypting and decrypting data. Managing these keys involves securely generating, distributing, and storing them to prevent compromise or unauthorized access. If encryption keys fall into the wrong hands, the entire encryption system can be rendered ineffective. Key management solutions (KMS) must therefore be meticulously designed to protect keys throughout their lifecycle—from generation to destruction.

Another concern involves the performance of cryptographic systems. Using encryption, particularly advanced methods, can significantly increase computational overhead, slowing down the encryption and decryption of large volumes of data. This can negatively impact the performance of systems processing personal data, especially in contexts like cloud computing or the IoT, where fast processing speeds are essential for a seamless user experience. Organizations must balance the use of robust cryptographic algorithms with the need for acceptable performance levels, which may require investments in specialized hardware or optimization technologies.

Regulatory compliance poses an additional challenge. Many regulations, such as the GDPR, mandate the adoption of adequate measures to protect personal data, including encryption. However, not all encryption methods are equally secure from a regulatory perspective. Some algorithms may not meet security standards or could become obsolete due to technological advancements. Organizations must ensure that the encryption algorithms they use comply with current regulations and are updated to withstand new threats. This requires constant vigilance and periodic upgrades to encryption solutions to prevent personal data from being secured with outdated methods.

Advanced encryption also presents usability and accessibility challenges. Implementing encryption can complicate data access for legitimate users, especially when additional authentication procedures or key management are required. For example, in a corporate setting, the use of individual encryption keys can increase the risk of data loss if an employee misplaces or forgets their key. Similarly, end-to-end encryption solutions, which ensure data remains encrypted throughout its transmission, can complicate access for authorized third parties, such as cloud service providers. Balancing data security with ease of access and system usability is thus a continuous challenge.

Finally, an emerging challenge for advanced encryption is the rise of quantum computing. Once fully developed, quantum computers could quickly decrypt many of the cryptographic algorithms currently in use. This means data encrypted with traditional technologies may not remain secure against this new form of computation. To address this threat, researchers are developing quantum-resistant cryptographic algorithms, but adopting these technologies on a large scale will take time and require significant infrastructure changes.

How can machine learning technologies improve the detection of privacy breaches?

Machine learning (ML) technologies have the potential to significantly enhance the detection of privacy breaches due to their ability to analyze large volumes of data quickly and accurately. Unlike traditional security systems based on fixed rules, ML systems can learn from data and adapt to new situations, making them highly effective in identifying anomalous or suspicious behavior that might be missed by other technologies.

One of the primary advantages of machine learning in detecting privacy breaches is its ability to analyze data flows and user activities in real time. ML systems can continuously monitor the behavior of users and devices within a network, identifying patterns of activity that deviate from the norm. For example, a machine learning system could detect unauthorized access to sensitive data, a sudden spike in requests for confidential information, or attempts to exfiltrate data. Anomalous behaviors can be quickly flagged to system administrators, who can intervene to block potential breaches before significant damage occurs.

Additionally, machine learning can improve privacy breach detection through the use of classification and clustering algorithms. These algorithms allow the system to automatically identify patterns of behavior associated with privacy breaches, such as unusual access to specific resources or abnormal data transfers. Clustering, in particular, is useful for grouping similar events and identifying activities that may seem harmless individually but constitute an attack when aggregated. In this way, ML systems can detect privacy violations that might not be immediately apparent through traditional methods.

A key strength of machine learning is its ability to improve over time. ML models can learn from new threats and update their detection capabilities as they encounter new types of attacks or breaches. This is particularly important in a context where privacy threats are constantly evolving and becoming increasingly sophisticated. For instance, machine learning can be used to detect new forms of phishing, social engineering, or data exfiltration attacks that were not anticipated when the system was first implemented.

Beyond detecting privacy breaches, machine learning can also be used to prevent them by improving access and authorization management. ML systems can analyze user behavior patterns to determine what types of access are typical for each user and which might represent a threat. For example, if an employee who usually accesses only specific documents suddenly requests access to sensitive files unrelated to their role, the ML system could flag this activity as suspicious.

Machine learning can also enhance privacy breach detection in the context of IoT technologies, where millions of interconnected devices continuously transmit data. In such scenarios, it is nearly impossible for network administrators to monitor all device activities manually. ML systems can automatically analyze the traffic generated by these devices, identifying anomalous behaviors that might indicate a privacy compromise or data breach. For example, a compromised IoT device might attempt to send large amounts of data to an unknown server, and an ML system could immediately detect and block this behavior.

However, using machine learning for privacy breach detection is not without challenges. One of the primary challenges is the need for high-quality, well-labeled datasets to train the models. Without sufficiently accurate data, ML models may produce false positives or fail to detect genuinely suspicious behavior. Another challenge is that while ML is highly effective at detecting anomalies, it may not always explain why a particular behavior was classified as a threat. This lack of transparency can make it difficult for system administrators to understand and address the root cause of breaches.

How does European regulation address personal data protection in IoT devices?

European regulation, particularly through the GDPR, addresses personal data protection in IoT devices with a focus on individual rights and the accountability of data processors. IoT devices, which include any internet-connected object capable of collecting, processing, and transmitting data, raise numerous privacy and security concerns. The GDPR provides a robust legal framework to ensure that personal data processed by such devices is adequately protected.

First, the principles of "privacy by design" and "privacy by default" require that devices be designed to collect only the data strictly necessary for their stated purposes and ensure that data is processed securely. Data collection must occur only when indispensable, and the default settings of devices must guarantee maximum privacy protection, avoiding excessive data collection.

Transparency is another key element of the GDPR that governs personal data protection in IoT devices. Manufacturers and operators must provide clear and comprehensible information to users about what data is collected, for what purposes, who will have access to it, and how long it will be retained. Users must be fully informed about how their data will be used and how they can exercise their rights, including the right to access,

rectify, or delete their data, as stipulated by the regulation.
The GDPR also imposes a strong obligation for informed consent. In the IoT context, users must be able to give explicit and informed consent before their data is collected and processed. This is particularly relevant for devices like wearables or voice assistants, which often collect sensitive personal data, including daily habits, geographic location, or even medical information. The regulation requires that consent be obtained clearly and unambiguously and that users can withdraw it at any time.
Another important tool provided by the GDPR is the Data Protection Impact Assessment (DPIA). This procedure must be conducted when the use of IoT devices could pose a high risk to individuals' rights and freedoms, such as when processing large-scale or particularly sensitive data. DPIAs help identify and mitigate risks before deploying the device or IoT system, ensuring that all necessary measures are taken to protect user privacy.
In addition to the GDPR, European regulation is evolving to keep pace with technological innovation. The forthcoming ePrivacy Regulation, currently under development, will complement the GDPR by providing more specific rules regarding privacy in electronic communications, including those related to the Internet of Things. This regulation aims to further strengthen personal data protection in areas such as behavioral advertising and online tracking, two domains closely linked to IoT devices.

What security measures are required for personal data in artificial intelligence systems?

The protection of personal data in artificial intelligence (AI) systems is critical, given that these systems often process vast amounts of information, including sensitive data. To ensure the secure management of personal data, European regulations mandate the implementation of a range of appropriate technical and organizational measures. These measures aim to prevent unauthorized access, loss, alteration, or improper disclosure of data. Below are some of the fundamental security measures required for personal data protection in AI systems.

Similar to traditional systems, encryption is a primary security measure, ensuring that information is protected during storage and transmission. Encryption renders data unreadable to anyone without authorization, thereby mitigating the risks of theft or breaches. In AI systems, where personal data may be processed in distributed environments or transmitted across various nodes, encryption is vital for maintaining data confidentiality.

Pseudonymization is another key technique used to process personal data in a way that it cannot be linked to a specific individual without additional information stored separately. In AI systems, pseudonymization reduces the risk of connecting processed data to users' real identities, protecting their privacy even in the event of unauthorized access to pseudonymized data.

Access limitation is an essential security measure in AI systems. Only authorized users and entities with legitimate purposes should access data. This requires strict access controls based on criteria such as multi-factor authentication (MFA) and the principle of least privilege, whereby users have access only to the information strictly necessary for their tasks.

Transparency in AI decision-making processes is also fundamental to ensuring personal data protection. Since many AI systems use complex algorithms to make automated decisions, these processes must be understandable and verifiable. This is not only necessary to comply with data protection regulations but also to allow users to understand how their personal data is processed.

Challenges related to transparency in AI systems are significant. If data processing involves non-deterministic decision-making layers, it can be difficult to reconstruct post hoc what occurred within the system. The recommended approach in such cases is to describe the system's features in advance, declare the presence of layers involving automated decisions, and present the design characteristics in a user-friendly manner. Users must be adequately informed to provide valid consent for data processing.

Organizations must also ensure continuous risk assessment for data security. AI systems are subject to rapidly evolving threats and vulnerabilities, making it essential to conduct periodic impact assessments of security measures. These assessments help identify and mitigate potential risks, ensuring that adopted security measures remain effective over time.

Secure key management is another required measure, involving the creation, distribution, and protection of keys used to encrypt and decrypt data. Poor key management can compromise the security of an entire system, leaving encrypted data vulnerable.

Continuous monitoring and log management are additional critical measures. AI systems must be monitored in real-time to detect and respond to potential security incidents, such as unauthorized access or anomalies in data processing. Activity logs must be securely maintained to enable auditing and verification of operations performed on personal data.

How can transparency in personal data usage be ensured with new technologies?

Transparency in the use of personal data is one of the fundamental principles enshrined in the GDPR and is increasingly challenging to achieve as technologies evolve. Ensuring transparency is essential to maintaining user trust and safeguarding their privacy rights. Transparency involves adequately informing users about how their data is collected, processed, and used, as well as providing them with meaningful control over these processes. To achieve this, organizations can adopt several strategies and measures.

First, one of the most effective ways to ensure transparency is to provide clear and accessible information to users about how their personal data is processed. Organizations must explain, in a comprehensible and concise manner, what data is collected, for what purposes, with whom it is shared, and how long it will be retained. These details must be presented simply, avoiding overly technical or legal jargon. Privacy notices should be designed to be easily understood by the average person, with straightforward explanations available through websites, apps, or other digital channels. Clarity is essential to enable users to make informed and conscious decisions about the processing of their personal data.

Second, to ensure transparency in personal data usage, organizations must obtain informed user consent before collecting and processing their data. The GDPR requires that consent be freely given, specific, informed, and unambiguous. This means users must clearly understand what they are consenting to and be able to refuse or withdraw consent at any time. The use of new technologies must not compromise users' rights to control their data. For instance, in applications of artificial intelligence or IoT, users should be able to easily manage their data preferences and receive notifications when their information is collected or processed.

Another way to ensure transparency is through traceability of data operations. Organizations can implement techniques that allow users to see how and when their data is used. Technologies like blockchain, for example, can create transparent and immutable records of transactions involving personal data. This allows users to verify which organizations have accessed their data and for what purposes. Traceability ensures that data is not used for purposes other than those initially declared.

Emerging technologies also require organizations to commit to greater explanation of automated decision-making processes. When personal data is processed by AI systems or machine learning algorithms, users must be informed about these processes and how automated decisions may affect them. For instance, if an algorithm determines whether an individual qualifies for a loan, the user must be made aware that a machine is making such decisions and has the right to request an explanation of the algorithm's logic.

To further strengthen transparency in personal data usage, organizations must ensure accountability and internal oversight. This includes appointing a Data Protection Officer (DPO), where required, and implementing internal policies for control and auditing to monitor how data is collected and used. Internal controls should be designed to ensure that all data processing activities comply with the GDPR and local privacy regulations.

3. CYBERSECURITY

What are the main certification requirements for the cybersecurity of digital products?

Cybersecurity certification for digital products is a fundamental process that ensures devices, software, and services are designed and implemented according to adequate security standards. In a context where cyber threats are increasingly pervasive and sophisticated, obtaining a cybersecurity certification demonstrates that a product has undergone rigorous testing and verification to ensure its security and reliability. At the European level, cybersecurity certification is evolving, particularly through the Cybersecurity Act, Regulation (EU) 2019/881, which introduced a common European framework for certifying digital products.

Under this regulation, one of the primary certification requirements for digital products is the evaluation of security risks. Companies must demonstrate that they have conducted a thorough assessment of potential threats that could compromise the product's security or the data it handles. This assessment identifies vulnerabilities and ensures the implementation of preventive measures such as encryption, access control, and protection against cyberattacks. Products must be designed to minimize vulnerabilities and withstand common threats, including malware, phishing, or direct attempts to breach defenses.

Another essential requirement is the adoption of technical security measures, including data protection through advanced encryption techniques, secure key management, and the use of secure communication protocols between devices. Additionally, digital products must include mechanisms for the secure management of software updates. The lack of regular updates or reliance on vulnerable systems is one of the main causes of successful cyberattacks. A key certification requirement is ensuring that the product can be updated securely and promptly without compromising system integrity.

Transparency is also a crucial aspect of cybersecurity certification. Digital product manufacturers must provide detailed documentation explaining the security measures adopted, update mechanisms, and vulnerability management processes. End users should be able to understand how the product's security is managed and what is being done to protect them from cyber threats. This transparency builds trust in the product and ensures that users are aware of the risks and protections available.

Effective vulnerability management is another critical requirement. Digital products must include a process for identifying and quickly addressing security flaws. This includes adopting patch management policies to ensure that vulnerabilities discovered after a product's release are fixed through software updates. The ability to respond swiftly to emerging threats is essential for maintaining a high level of security.

Finally, product resilience against attacks is a key consideration. A certified product must demonstrate the ability to continue functioning even in the presence of attacks or malfunctions. This capacity to withstand or quickly recover from an attack is crucial for products used in healthcare, financial services, or critical infrastructure. Resilience testing is often part of the certification process to ensure that the product can handle unforeseen events without compromising data or system security.

How do new European regulations improve the response to cybersecurity incidents?

New European regulations have introduced significant measures to improve the response to cybersecurity incidents by strengthening the protection of digital infrastructures and ensuring that organizations are better prepared to prevent, manage, and respond to such incidents. In addition to the GDPR, the NIS2 Directive is among the most relevant regulations, establishing clear guidelines and obligations for organizations to ensure a timely and effective reaction to threats and cyberattacks.

The NIS2 Directive (Network and Information Systems Directive), which updates the previous NIS Directive, represents a major step forward in improving the response to cybersecurity incidents in Europe. The directive applies to critical infrastructures and essential sectors, such as transportation, healthcare, energy, and financial services, imposing stringent requirements for cybersecurity management. One of its most significant measures is the obligation for organizations to implement incident management plans and conduct regular testing of their response capabilities. These plans must include detailed procedures for detecting, analyzing, containing, and mitigating the effects of a security incident, as well as for restoring normal operations. This ensures that organizations are prepared to respond to attacks in a coordinated and systematic manner.

The new European regulations also promote international and cross-sectoral cooperation in managing cybersecurity incidents. The NIS2 Directive mandates the establishment of national contact points that collaborate with other EU Member States to share information about incidents and coordinate responses at a cross-border level. This integrated approach allows for more efficient handling of cyber threats, as large-scale attacks affecting multiple countries can be addressed more effectively through better information sharing and resource allocation.

Another feature of the new European regulations is the requirement to adopt proactive and preventive measures to reduce the risk of cybersecurity incidents. For example, the NIS2 Directive requires organizations to implement state-of-the-art cybersecurity practices, including risk management, advanced defense technologies, and personnel training. These proactive measures not only reduce the likelihood of incidents but also ensure that organizations are better equipped to respond effectively when cyberattacks occur.

The NIS2 Directive also includes substantial penalties for organizations that fail to comply with cybersecurity requirements or adequately respond to incidents. Fines can be significant, in some cases reaching up to 2% of an organization's global annual turnover. This compliance obligation serves as a strong incentive for organizations to improve their defenses and ensure they can respond to security incidents promptly and effectively.

How can artificial intelligence technologies be used to improve cybersecurity?

Artificial intelligence (AI) technologies hold immense potential for enhancing cybersecurity due to their ability to analyze large volumes of data quickly, detect emerging threats, and automate responses to attacks. AI can be leveraged in various ways to strengthen cyber defenses and reduce response times, making security systems more proactive and effective.

One of the main advantages of AI in cybersecurity is its ability to detect threats in real time. AI systems can continuously monitor vast data streams and identify anomalous behaviors that may indicate an ongoing cyberattack. Using machine learning algorithms, these systems can learn from past threats and improve their ability to recognize suspicious activities over time. For instance, AI can detect unusual login patterns, such as a sudden surge of access attempts from unusual locations or unauthorized users. This early detection capability allows organizations to act before significant damage occurs.

AI can also enhance vulnerability management by analyzing systems to identify potential security flaws, such as outdated software or misconfigurations, and suggesting appropriate fixes. Additionally, by analyzing data from diverse sources, AI can predict which vulnerabilities are most likely to be exploited by attackers, enabling organizations to focus on protecting critical weak points.

Another critical application of AI is automating incident response. AI can be programmed to automatically trigger countermeasures in response to specific threats, such as blocking a suspicious IP address or isolating a compromised system. Automation reduces response times, minimizing potential impact. Security Information and Event Management (SIEM) technologies, which combine data collection on security events with advanced analysis capabilities, have significantly benefited from AI integration. These systems can generate more accurate alerts and reduce false positives, allowing security teams to focus on genuine threats.

AI is also valuable in combating zero-day attacks, which exploit previously unknown vulnerabilities without existing patches or solutions. Machine learning algorithms can identify abnormal behaviors that suggest the use of unknown exploits, enabling attacks to be blocked even before the vulnerability is discovered. This capability to address yet-unknown threats is particularly valuable as cybercriminals continuously develop new attack techniques.

AI can further improve identity protection through advanced authentication systems. For instance, AI technologies can analyze user behavior and detect suspicious authentication patterns, such as changes in access habits or unusual device usage. These systems can strengthen multi-factor authentication, requiring additional verifications only when atypical behavior is detected.

AI is also effective in preventing phishing attacks. AI systems can analyze the content of emails, messages, and websites to identify phishing attempts, flagging suspicious communications or blocking access to potentially malicious sites. Machine learning algorithms can learn from previous phishing patterns and recognize new variants of these attacks, continuously improving their ability to protect against similar threats in the future.

While AI offers numerous cybersecurity benefits, it also faces challenges. Training algorithms requires large amounts of high-quality data. Without sufficiently representative data, models may fail to detect threats accurately or produce excessive false positives. Moreover, cybercriminals might attempt to manipulate data to deceive AI systems and evade detection. Therefore, securing AI systems themselves against potential manipulations is crucial.

What are the main vulnerabilities of IoT systems in terms of cybersecurity?

IoT systems are transforming numerous sectors by connecting smart devices that communicate with each other and global networks. However, this continuous connectivity and the widespread adoption of IoT devices expose these systems to a wide range of vulnerabilities, making them attractive targets for cybercriminals. The fragmented and often heterogeneous nature of the IoT ecosystem, coupled with the lack of uniform security standards, creates several weaknesses that must be addressed to improve overall security.

A primary vulnerability of IoT systems is the poor security built into many devices. Many devices are developed with a strong focus on functionality and ease of use, often at the expense of security. For instance, many IoT devices do not implement adequate authentication protocols or use default passwords that are easily guessed. These weaknesses enable attackers to access IoT devices with relative ease, compromising the network or exploiting devices to launch distributed attacks such as Distributed Denial of Service (DDoS) attacks.

Another common vulnerability is the lack of updates and security patches. Many IoT devices are not designed to receive regular software updates, meaning that once a vulnerability is discovered, the device may remain exposed for a long time. Even when updates are available, users are often not adequately informed or incentivized to install them. This issue is exacerbated by the fact that some IoT devices have relatively long lifespans, but the manufacturer's support may end before the device's operational life does, leaving it unprotected and exposed to new threats.

A critical vulnerability in IoT systems is the lack of encryption for transmitted data. Many IoT devices transmit sensitive data without employing adequate encryption measures, making information vulnerable during transmission. Without encryption, data can be intercepted or altered by unauthorized third parties, exposing users to privacy breaches or data manipulation. For example, devices such as security cameras or smart thermostats lacking encryption may allow attackers to intercept personal data or alter device settings.

Inadequate network segmentation is another weak point in IoT systems. Many IoT devices are connected to the same network used by computers and other critical devices, creating a significant security risk. If a single IoT device is compromised, attackers could use it as an entry point to access other parts of the network and launch broader attacks, jeopardizing the entire infrastructure. Insufficient or non-existent network segmentation allows attackers to expand their reach once they infiltrate the system through a vulnerable device.

The limited processing power of many IoT devices is another vulnerability. Due to their often compact and low-cost nature, many devices lack the capacity to implement robust security algorithms. This limitation prevents the use of advanced encryption or more secure authentication technologies. Additionally, the absence of monitoring and intrusion detection capabilities within the devices themselves makes it challenging for users to know if a device has been compromised or is being maliciously used.

Poor user awareness is another factor contributing to the vulnerabilities of IoT systems. Many consumers do not fully understand the risks associated with using IoT devices and often fail to change default security settings such as passwords or network configurations. This behavior can facilitate unauthorized access to devices and increase the risk of compromise. Moreover, many users are unaware of the importance of software updates or additional protective measures.

Lastly, the lack of standardization and regulation cannot be overlooked. The IoT market is fragmented, with a wide range of manufacturers offering devices with varying security standards. The absence of standardization means that devices are not subject to the same security requirements, creating a disjointed environment where less secure devices can compromise the overall security of an IoT system.

How can critical infrastructures be protected from cyber threats?

Critical infrastructures—including energy systems, telecommunications networks, transportation, healthcare, and financial services—are essential for the functioning of modern society and must be protected from an increasing variety of cyber threats. As these infrastructures become increasingly digitalized and interconnected, they become attractive targets for cyberattacks, which could cause significant damage in terms of service disruptions, economic losses, and risks to public safety. Protecting these infrastructures from cyber threats requires a multilayered approach involving technical, organizational, and regulatory measures.

One of the fundamental pillars for protecting critical infrastructures is the implementation of robust cybersecurity measures at the technological level. These measures include network segmentation, encryption to protect sensitive data, advanced firewalls, intrusion detection and prevention systems (IDS/IPS), and multifactor authentication solutions. Network segmentation, in particular, is necessary to limit lateral movement by attackers within an infrastructure: isolating critical systems in separate networks reduces the risk that an attack on one part of the infrastructure compromises the entire system. Additionally, the use of advanced monitoring techniques, such as artificial intelligence and machine learning, enables the detection of suspicious activities in real-time and quick responses to security incidents.

Training and raising awareness among personnel are another key element in protecting critical infrastructures. Cyberattacks often exploit human errors, such as opening phishing emails or downloading malicious attachments. Providing continuous training to employees on cyber risks and best practices to avoid attacks significantly reduces the risk of incidents. Organizations should also simulate cyberattacks, such as phishing exercises or penetration tests, to evaluate staff readiness and improve their ability to respond to threats.

Another essential tool for protecting critical infrastructures is the adoption of business continuity and crisis management plans. These plans must include strategies to ensure that critical systems continue to function even in the event of cyberattacks. Regular backups and redundancy of key systems are fundamental components of a business continuity plan, enabling rapid restoration of operations in the event of a disaster. A crisis management plan must clearly define the roles and responsibilities of personnel during an attack, as well as internal and external communication procedures to reduce response times and mitigate the impact of the attack.

Collaboration between the public and private sectors is another essential component for protecting critical infrastructures. Since many critical infrastructures are managed by private entities, it is crucial for these actors to collaborate with government authorities and share information on threats and attacks. In Europe, the NIS2 Directive requires greater collaboration between member states and companies managing critical infrastructures to improve resilience and incident response. Cooperation involves sharing threat information, standardizing security procedures, and creating secure communication networks for crisis management.

Continuous risk assessment and management are crucial

to ensuring that critical infrastructures can withstand new threats. Organizations must regularly conduct cybersecurity risk assessments to identify potential vulnerabilities and determine the necessary countermeasures to reduce risk. This assessment process must be dynamic, as cyber threats evolve rapidly. Effective risk management involves not only mitigating technical vulnerabilities but also assessing human and organizational factors that could expose the infrastructure to threats.

It is also important to adopt internationally recognized security standards and certifications. Standards such as ISO/IEC 27001, which establishes requirements for information security management systems, provide organizations with a framework for implementing solid and consistent security measures. Compliance with such standards ensures that critical infrastructures follow best security practices and are prepared to respond to threats effectively. Not to mention that some regulations, such as the European Union Cybersecurity Act, require cybersecurity certification for products and services, thereby encouraging organizations to continuously improve their defenses.

What are the security requirements for cloud computing platforms according to new European guidelines?

The new European regulations define a set of specific security requirements for cloud computing platforms, aiming to ensure the protection of personal data and the resilience of critical infrastructures. These requirements focus on aspects such as data protection, vulnerability management, operational continuity, and regulatory compliance.

The European General Data Protection Regulation (GDPR) stipulates that cloud service providers must adopt adequate technical and organizational measures to ensure the security of processed data. This includes the use of encryption techniques to protect data during transmission and storage, the implementation of pseudonymization measures, and the adoption of data minimization policies to collect only the data strictly necessary for the declared purpose. Cloud computing platforms must guarantee that personal data is processed in compliance with the rights of data subjects, ensuring that organizations using cloud services can easily exercise rights such as data access, rectification, and deletion.

Another fundamental requirement concerns access management. Cloud platforms must implement strict controls to ensure that only authorized personnel have access to personal data or sensitive resources. Multifactor authentication is often required to protect user accounts from unauthorized access, while adopting the principle of least privilege ensures that users have access only to the information and resources necessary to perform their tasks.

Operational continuity is another critical aspect regulated by European standards, particularly the NIS2 Directive, which requires cloud platforms to adopt crisis management and business continuity plans. These plans must ensure that cloud services can continue to operate even in the event of security incidents or malfunctions, minimizing downtime and impact on business activities. Cloud platforms must implement redundancy measures such as regular data backups and the geographic distribution of resources to ensure data availability even in the event of physical failures or cyberattacks.

A critical security requirement for cloud computing platforms is vulnerability and update management. Cloud platforms must be able to quickly detect and address security vulnerabilities through timely updates and patches. Additionally, it is essential to implement a continuous monitoring system to identify potential threats or anomalies that may indicate the presence of an attack. Failure to update known vulnerabilities is one of the main security risks, which is why European regulations emphasize the adoption of proactive vulnerability management practices.

Transparency and traceability of operations are also key requirements for cloud platforms. Service providers must ensure that their customers have visibility into how data is processed, where it is stored, and who has access to it. Logging access and data processing operations is fundamental to ensuring transparency. These logs must be securely stored to enable audits and inspections by competent authorities. Additionally, cloud platforms must provide their customers with detailed information on the security measures adopted and on any security incidents that could compromise data or services.

Finally, compliance with European regulations and international security standards is another fundamental requirement. Cloud computing platforms must ensure that their infrastructures and processes comply not only with the GDPR and the NIS2 Directive but also with international security standards such as ISO/IEC 27001. Certification of compliance with international standards is often an essential requirement to attract customers and build trust in cloud services.

How can blockchain technologies improve the security of digital transactions?

Blockchain technologies offer numerous advantages for the security of digital transactions, thanks to their intrinsic characteristics of decentralization, immutability, and transparency. These features make blockchain an ideal solution to address many of the security challenges associated with digital transactions across various sectors, such as finance, logistics, and identity management.

Unlike traditional systems, where transactions are managed and validated by a single centralized entity, blockchain operates on a distributed network of nodes working together to verify transactions. Each node in the network holds an up-to-date copy of the transaction ledger, significantly reducing the risk of cyberattacks, as there is no single point of vulnerability that can be compromised. Decentralization makes digital transactions more secure because to manipulate or compromise a transaction, an attacker would need to simultaneously control most of the network nodes—an extremely challenging task in a well-distributed blockchain network.

Another key feature of blockchain is data immutability. Once a transaction is recorded on a blockchain, it becomes practically impossible to modify or delete due to cryptographic algorithms and the structure of the chain of blocks. Each block is linked to the previous one through a cryptographic hash that ensures the integrity of the recorded data. If someone attempts to alter a transaction, the entire chain is disrupted, making the alteration immediately evident. This guarantees the security and integrity of digital transactions, as users can be certain that the data recorded on the blockchain cannot be retroactively modified.

Transparency in blockchain further enhances the security of digital transactions. In a public blockchain, all transactions are visible to all participants in the network, making it much harder to hide fraudulent activities. Although user identities are generally pseudonymized or encrypted, the transparency of the public ledger ensures that all transactions can be tracked and verified by anyone. This increases trust in the system, as users can independently verify the integrity of transactions and ensure there have been no attempts at fraud or manipulation.

The use of smart contracts also enhances the security of digital transactions. Smart contracts are self-executing programs recorded on a blockchain that automatically activate when specific conditions are met. These are secure and immutable digital contracts that do not require intermediaries for execution. Smart contracts can ensure that transactions only occur when all the specified conditions in the contract are fulfilled, reducing the risk of fraud or human error. Moreover, being executed in a decentralized environment, they offer a high level of security as they cannot be altered or tampered with after their creation.

Resilience to DDoS attacks is another advantage that blockchain offers over centralized systems. Since blockchain operates on a distributed network, there is no single point of failure that can be targeted by DDoS attacks, which aim to overload a server with excessive requests. In a blockchain network, even if one node is attacked or compromised, the other nodes continue to function normally, ensuring that transactions can proceed without interruption—significantly increasing the security and resilience of digital transactions against such attacks.

Blockchain also significantly improves identity protection during digital transactions. It enables the use of pseudonymization or cryptographic techniques to protect user identities, reducing the risk of identity theft or unauthorized access to personal data. This is especially critical in sectors such as finance or healthcare, where protecting user privacy is paramount.

Finally, blockchain enhances the security of digital transactions by reducing reliance on intermediaries. In traditional systems, transactions often require the presence of trusted third parties, such as banks or financial institutions, to verify and guarantee their validity. However, these intermediaries also represent points of vulnerability, as they can be targets of cyberattacks or internal fraud. Blockchain eliminates the need for these intermediaries, as transactions are validated directly by the decentralized network and consensus mechanisms. This not only reduces costs associated with intermediaries but also removes potential weak points in transaction security.

What are the cybersecurity challenges in connected medical devices?

Connected medical devices, such as pacemakers, infusion pumps, remote monitoring devices, and wearable technologies, have revolutionized healthcare by providing new tools for patient management and treatment. However, these devices introduce significant cybersecurity challenges because they handle extremely sensitive data and interact directly with the health and lives of individuals. Connecting these devices to networks, hospitals, or personal devices exposes them to substantial risks, making cybersecurity a critical priority in the healthcare sector.

One of the primary concerns is the protection of personal and sensitive data. Connected medical devices collect and transmit personal and medical information about patients, such as biometric data, medical history, and treatment details. These data are valuable to cybercriminals, as they can be used for fraud, extortion, or sale on the dark web. Ensuring that the data transmitted by these devices are protected against unauthorized access through encryption and secure communication protocols is fundamental to preventing privacy breaches.

Another critical challenge is the security of the devices themselves. Many connected medical devices are designed to operate for extended periods, often without regular updates or security patches. This makes them vulnerable to known exploits or new threats that emerge during their operational lifetime. Manufacturers of medical devices often prioritize clinical performance and ease of use over cybersecurity during the design phase. The lack of updates and adequate security measures can leave devices susceptible to compromise, putting patient safety at risk.

The complexity of hospital networks poses another issue for the cybersecurity of connected medical devices. Modern healthcare infrastructures use a vast array of interconnected devices and systems that communicate over often complex and fragmented networks. A connected medical device that is not sufficiently secure can serve as an entry point for attackers, leading to the compromise of the entire hospital network. Hospital networks are particularly vulnerable to ransomware attacks, where cybercriminals encrypt data or block access to medical systems until a ransom is paid. A connected medical device could be exploited to facilitate such an attack.

Managing authorizations and access is another critical

challenge. Many connected medical devices require access from various parties, including healthcare providers, patients, and maintenance technicians, to monitor and manage their functions. Ensuring that only authorized individuals have access to the data or critical functions of the device is essential to prevent unauthorized access. Weak authentication systems or the use of easily compromised credentials could allow malicious actors to access and manipulate the device, potentially endangering patients' health.

Physical security of connected medical devices, particularly those that are wearable or implantable and in constant contact with patients, is another priority. Preventing potential tampering or unauthorized physical access is essential. For instance, an attacker could attempt to interfere with a medical device to alter its functionality or disable it entirely. Ensuring that devices are designed to be physically secure and resistant to tampering is critical to preventing such threats.

Interoperability and compatibility among connected medical devices are also significant concerns. Often, devices come from different manufacturers and must be integrated into a unified healthcare system. Differences in security protocols or software solutions can create vulnerabilities. If one device does not adhere to the same security standards as others in the ecosystem, it could become the weak link through which an attacker gains access to the network. Adopting common and interoperable security standards in healthcare is essential to reducing the risk of compromise.

In Europe, the General Data Protection Regulation (GDPR) imposes strict standards for protecting personal data, which apply to the data processed by medical devices. However, specific regulations on the cybersecurity of medical devices are still under development. It is essential that device manufacturers and healthcare facilities comply with existing regulations and prepare to meet upcoming requirements, such as the NIS2 Directive, which includes provisions for the security of healthcare infrastructures.

How can the security of 5G networks be ensured?

5G networks are one of the most significant innovations in telecommunications, offering much higher connection speeds, lower latency, and greater capacity to support connected devices compared to previous generations. However, the introduction of 5G networks also presents new security challenges due to their architectural complexity, heavy reliance on software, and the growing number of connected devices, including critical ones like medical devices, autonomous vehicles, and industrial infrastructure. Ensuring the security of 5G networks is therefore essential to mitigate risks that could compromise both user privacy and infrastructure stability.

A key step in ensuring the security of 5G networks is implementing integrated security measures at the design and infrastructure levels. Security must be considered from the earliest stages of network design, following the principle of "security by design." This involves embedding security technologies directly into the infrastructure to ensure that every network component, from software to hardware, is protected against cyber threats. For example, advanced encryption must be used to secure data transmitted over the network, and connected devices must support robust authentication protocols to prevent unauthorized access.

Network segmentation is another measure that enhances the security of 5G networks. The virtualized structure of 5G allows it to be divided into segments or "slices," each of which can be isolated and configured differently based on security requirements and the applications it supports. This approach ensures better protection for devices and data depending on their level of risk. For instance, networks supporting critical infrastructures like healthcare or energy services can be separated from those supporting less sensitive applications, reducing exposure to security risks and ensuring that an attack on one segment does not compromise the entire network.

The use of Network Function Virtualization (NFV) and Software-Defined Networks (SDN) in 5G provides significant advantages in terms of flexibility and scalability but also introduces security challenges. These technologies allow dynamic network management and control through software, removing many traditional hardware barriers. However, a vulnerability in the network management software could expose the entire network to risks. To mitigate these risks, advanced security solutions such as virtualized firewalls, intrusion detection systems, and automated segmentation mechanisms must be implemented to protect data flows and detect anomalies in real time.

Another critical aspect of securing 5G networks is protecting devices from attacks. With the expansion of the Internet of Things (IoT) and the increasing connectivity of mobile devices, the attack surface for 5G networks has significantly increased. It is therefore essential to ensure that all connected devices comply with high security standards, using secure authentication mechanisms, encryption, and malware protection. Device manufacturers must provide regular updates to address potential vulnerabilities and ensure that devices can be managed securely within the network.

Collaboration between service providers and public authorities is also vital for securing 5G networks. These networks are critical infrastructure, requiring cooperation between governments and telecommunications operators to establish clear security standards and share information about emerging threats. However, this task is challenging, especially in the context of global tensions where states and their organizations are engaged in hybrid warfare. In such scenarios, network infrastructures can become both targets and tools for attacking adversaries.

This is why the European Union's NIS2 Directive requires operators of critical infrastructures, including 5G service providers, to adopt strict security measures and participate in sharing information about cyber threats.

What are best practices for managing vulnerabilities in Software as a Service (SaaS)?

Managing vulnerabilities in Software as a Service (SaaS) applications is critical to ensuring the security of applications and protecting user data from potential cyber threats. Because the SaaS model involves delivering software through the cloud, vulnerabilities in these services can have wide-ranging impacts and simultaneously affect numerous users.

The first essential practice is identifying and managing vulnerabilities. SaaS providers must implement a continuous process to scan for vulnerabilities in their software. This includes using automated security tools to analyze source code, as well as assessing configurations and dependencies used within the software. Continuous monitoring helps to identify new vulnerabilities before they can be exploited by cybercriminals. Adopting bug bounty programs, where external security experts are incentivized to find flaws in the system, is another effective strategy for uncovering undetected vulnerabilities.

A second key practice is the rapid application of security patches. Once a vulnerability is identified, it is crucial to develop and deploy security patches promptly. In the SaaS context, software updates can be implemented in real time, significantly reducing risks associated with lingering vulnerabilities. Providers must ensure that patch management processes are well-defined and automated to avoid delays in implementing security solutions. Additionally, timely notifications to customers about discovered vulnerabilities and corrective actions improve transparency and build trust in the service.

Securing software dependencies is another critical area in SaaS vulnerability management. Many SaaS applications rely on open-source components or third-party libraries, making it essential to continuously monitor these dependencies for known vulnerabilities. Companies should use dependency management tools to automatically identify vulnerable library versions and provide alerts about available updates. Avoiding unnecessary dependencies and limiting the integration of third-party packages can also reduce potential points of vulnerability. Implementing a Secure Software Development Lifecycle (SSDLC) is another best practice. Integrating security practices into the software development lifecycle ensures that security is considered at every stage of SaaS application development. This includes adopting secure coding practices, conducting code reviews, penetration testing, and validating vulnerabilities during the design, development, and deployment phases. The SSDLC helps prevent the introduction of vulnerabilities and ensures that applications are built with security as a top priority. Segmentation and data separation are also essential for managing vulnerabilities in SaaS. Because SaaS services often host data from multiple clients on the same infrastructure, ensuring proper isolation and separation of data for each client is critical. Segmentation can be achieved through containerization or secure virtualization environments, ensuring that a vulnerability in one service instance cannot be exploited to access other clients' data. This approach limits the potential impact of an attack and protects data privacy.

Employee training is equally important in vulnerability management. Development and infrastructure teams must be trained on the best security practices and the latest techniques for detecting and addressing vulnerabilities. Continuous training on emerging threats and security tools ensures that SaaS organizations are always prepared to manage new vulnerabilities effectively. Moreover, fostering a culture of security across the organization encourages greater attention to data protection and vulnerability management.

Finally, using threat monitoring and detection tools is one of the best practices for managing vulnerabilities in SaaS software. Real-time monitoring solutions and artificial intelligence can help detect abnormal behaviors or suspicious activities in SaaS systems. These tools can identify potential vulnerabilities and ongoing attacks, enabling security teams to respond quickly and mitigate risks. Combining threat detection tools with automated incident response systems enhances the ability to prevent or limit damage from exploiting vulnerabilities.

4. PHYSICAL SAFETY OF WORKERS

How can new technologies improve worker physical safety in the manufacturing industry?

New technologies offer numerous opportunities to enhance the physical safety of workers in the manufacturing industry, a sector historically characterized by potentially hazardous work environments. From automation to advanced robotics, and from wearable devices to sensors, technological innovations are contributing to creating safer workplaces, reducing accident risks, improving monitoring of workers' physical conditions, and optimizing safety management processes.

One of the main technological tools revolutionizing safety in the manufacturing sector is the use of collaborative robotics, or cobots. Cobots are robots designed to work alongside humans, assisting workers in repetitive, heavy, or dangerous tasks. Thanks to advanced sensors and AI algorithms, cobots can detect the presence of workers and immediately halt their activities in case of risk, drastically reducing accidents caused by accidental contact with moving machinery. Additionally, cobots' ability to perform physically demanding tasks helps prevent musculoskeletal injuries, one of the most common problems in the manufacturing sector.

Another significant contribution to worker safety comes from wearable technologies, such as smart helmets and vests. These devices can be equipped with sensors capable of monitoring workers' physical conditions in real time, including heart rate, body temperature, and fatigue levels. By analyzing the collected data, early signs of physical stress or exhaustion can be identified before they pose a threat to the worker's health. In case of anomalies, wearable devices can send notifications to supervisors or central systems, triggering preventive measures such as mandatory breaks or medical intervention.

Internet of Things (IoT) solutions are also revolutionizing physical safety in manufacturing. IoT enables the creation of interconnected networks of devices that continuously monitor and control the work environment. For example, sensors along a production line can detect the presence of hazardous chemicals, toxic gases, or abnormal temperatures, immediately alerting workers and safety personnel. This type of continuous and automated monitoring reduces the need for manual inspections, which are often dangerous, and allows for quick responses to emergencies, minimizing risks to workers' safety.

Another important technological development involves the use of augmented reality (AR) and virtual reality (VR) for training and accident prevention. Through realistic simulations, workers can be trained on how to handle emergencies or operate in high-risk environments without being exposed to danger. VR allows workers to practice critical work scenarios, such as maintaining heavy machinery or evacuating during a fire, while AR can provide real-time visual instructions directly on-site, for example, during the inspection or repair of complex equipment. This immersive training helps workers better understand safety procedures and face real-world situations with greater confidence.

Additionally, artificial intelligence technologies, particularly machine learning algorithms, are being used to improve worker safety through predictive analysis. These systems analyze historical data on incidents and factory risks to identify patterns and trends that may indicate potential future risks. For instance, AI can predict when a machine is likely to fail based on maintenance and usage data, allowing for scheduled preventive maintenance. This reduces the risk of sudden breakdowns that could cause accidents or harm to workers.

Finally, drones are improving worker physical safety in manufacturing. Drones are used to inspect hard-to-reach or hazardous areas, such as elevated structures or confined spaces.

They can collect detailed images and data without exposing workers to risks, providing real-time information to safety personnel.

What are the safety requirements for machinery under Directive 2006/42/EC, and what changes with Regulation (EU) 2023/1230?

Directive 2006/42/EC, also known as the Machinery Directive, provides the main regulatory framework in the European Union to ensure the safety of machinery in the single market. The directive establishes essential safety and health requirements that must be met during the design, manufacturing, and use of machinery. With the entry into force of Regulation (EU) 2023/1230 in January 2027, which replaces the directive, significant updates and changes have been introduced to modernize and strengthen the regulations in line with technological advancements.

Under Directive 2006/42/EC, machinery must be designed and constructed to ensure safety for its intended use and to prevent risks to the health and safety of individuals during installation, operation, cleaning, maintenance, and dismantling.

The main safety requirements include:

General Safety and Health Requirements
Machinery must be designed to prevent safety risks, such as entrapment, injuries caused by moving parts, electric shocks, exposure to hazardous substances, or excessive noise. Protective measures and barriers must be provided to prevent accidental contact with dangerous components.

Emergency Controls
The directive requires machinery to be equipped with easily accessible emergency devices, such as stop buttons, that allow

rapid shutdown in case of imminent danger. Additionally, machinery must be capable of visually or audibly signaling any abnormal or hazardous conditions.

Ergonomics and Ease of Use
Machinery must be designed with ergonomic principles in mind to minimize injury risks from human errors. They must feature intuitive and user-friendly control interfaces, enabling operators to use them without difficulty or confusion.

The directive requires manufacturers to provide comprehensive technical documentation, including user manuals, operational schematics, and maintenance information. Machines must bear the CE marking, which certifies compliance with the safety and health requirements established by the directive. Manufacturers are responsible for assessing the machinery's conformity before it is placed on the market.
With the entry into force of Regulation (EU) 2023/1230, significant updates have been made to address the challenges posed by digitalization and emerging technologies such as artificial intelligence and advanced automation.

Cybersecurity Requirements
One of the most notable changes in Regulation 2023/1230 is the inclusion of cybersecurity requirements. With the increasing use of connected machinery and digital control systems, the new regulation requires machines to be protected against cybersecurity risks. This includes measures to prevent unauthorized access to control systems and protection against cyberattacks that could compromise safe operation.

Requirements for Autonomous and AI-Based Machinery
The regulation introduces specific standards for machines integrating advanced technologies such as AI or operating autonomously. These machines must be designed to ensure that their control algorithms are safe and do not

introduce unforeseen risks to health and safety. Additionally, manufacturers must ensure that such machines can detect and respond to emergency conditions without requiring human intervention.

Advanced Harmonized Standards
The regulation encourages the adoption of more advanced harmonized technical standards, aligning with new technologies and best practices for machinery design. This includes promoting standards for secure connectivity, integrating automation systems, and managing safe human-machine interfaces.

Enhanced Manufacturer and Economic Operator Responsibility
The new regulation reinforces obligations for manufacturers, distributors, and importers, mandating not only the compliance of machinery with safety standards but also ongoing monitoring of safety performance after the product is released on the market. This includes obligations to report safety-related incidents immediately and update machines, if necessary, to resolve vulnerabilities.

Improved Transparency and Traceability
The regulation introduces new measures to enhance transparency and traceability throughout the supply chain. Manufacturers must ensure more detailed and accessible documentation on machinery compliance and safety, facilitating evaluations by control authorities and end users.

How can smart sensors be used to prevent workplace accidents?

Smart sensors are among the most innovative and promising technologies for preventing workplace accidents, especially in high-risk industries such as manufacturing, construction, and transportation. Equipped with advanced functionalities such as real-time monitoring, data collection and analysis, and the ability to communicate with other devices via IoT networks, these sensors enable the detection of hazardous conditions and timely interventions to prevent accidents and ensure worker safety.

First, smart sensors can be used to monitor the work environment and detect dangerous conditions before an accident occurs. For example, temperature, humidity, pressure, and gas detectors can be installed in industrial plants or construction sites to continuously monitor the environment and send alerts if hazardous conditions are detected, such as the presence of toxic gasses, extreme temperatures, or abnormal pressure variations. These sensors can trigger immediate alarms, notifying workers and safety personnel to evacuate the area or take appropriate protective measures.

Another critical use of smart sensors involves monitoring workers' physical conditions. Wearable devices equipped with biometric sensors, such as smart wristbands or vests with sensors, can monitor vital parameters like heart rate, blood oxygen levels, body temperature, and blood pressure. These data can help identify signs of fatigue, physical stress, dehydration, or exposure to toxic environments, all factors that increase the risk of workplace accidents. If a sensor detects a high heart rate or signs of fatigue in a worker, the system can alert supervisors, suggesting a break before fatigue leads to errors or accidents.

Smart sensors also enhance machine safety and prevent accidents by monitoring equipment conditions. Sensors installed on machines and tools can detect anomalies in their operation, such as excessive vibrations, component wear, or changes in power output. These data can be used to perform predictive maintenance, preventing sudden failures that could lead to serious accidents. For instance, if a sensor detects abnormal vibration increases in a machine, it could indicate that a mechanical part is deteriorating and needs replacement before a failure endangers workers.

Another effective use of smart sensors is proximity and motion detection. In industries where workers operate near heavy machinery or industrial vehicles such as cranes or forklifts, proximity sensors can detect the presence of people or objects near the machinery and send alerts to the operator or control system. Industrial vehicles can be equipped with automatic stop systems that activate when they detect people too close. This type of technology drastically reduces accidents involving people coming into contact with moving machinery.

Smart sensors can also be employed to ensure safety in confined or hazardous areas. Position and motion sensors can track the exact location of workers within a workspace and detect if someone gets too close to a dangerous area, such as an unprotected edge or a high-risk zone where hazardous chemicals are handled. In such cases, the system can emit an audible or visual warning to alert the worker to the danger and, if necessary, send a signal to the central system to halt nearby activities or machinery.

Vision-based technologies and AI-powered sensors further enhance worker safety. Intelligent camera systems combined with AI algorithms can continuously monitor workers' movements and detect hazardous behaviors or risk situations, such as falls, slips, or incorrect postures when using heavy tools. Finally, smart sensors play a crucial role in emergency management. In case of incidents such as fires or explosions, sensors installed in a work area can automatically activate alarm and evacuation systems. Additionally, real-time location systems (RTLS) sensors can track the exact positions of workers during an emergency, aiding rescuers in quickly finding and assisting those in hazardous situations.

What are the implications of advanced robotics on worker safety?

The implications of advanced robotics on worker safety are broad and complex. While this technology offers numerous advantages in terms of efficiency and productivity, it also introduces new challenges for workplace safety. The integration of advanced robotics, including cobots, autonomous robots, and automated systems, is radically transforming how many industrial and operational tasks are performed, directly impacting workers' health and safety.

One of the primary advantages of advanced robotics is reducing workers' exposure to physical risks. Robots can be deployed to perform dangerous, heavy, or repetitive tasks, minimizing human involvement in operations that carry a high risk of injury. For instance, robots can operate in extreme environments such as hot, cold, or toxic settings found in foundries, chemical plants, or mines. This shields workers from conditions that could otherwise cause illnesses or injuries. Advanced robotics also facilitates lifting heavy loads or performing precision tasks that would be difficult or dangerous for humans, reducing musculoskeletal injury risks.

However, the increasing automation and presence of autonomous robots in workplaces bring new challenges, particularly regarding human-robot interaction safety. Advanced robots, especially cobots, are designed to work alongside humans, but close interaction can pose risks if safety systems are inadequate. Failures in proximity sensors or errors in the robot's control algorithm could lead to collisions with workers or unexpected robot behavior, resulting in injuries. To minimize such risks, cobots must be equipped with sophisticated sensors capable of accurately detecting human presence and immediately adjusting their speed or halting operations in case of danger.

Another significant implication of advanced robotics is the need for specialized worker training. While introducing robots may reduce physically demanding tasks for workers, it also necessitates higher technical skills. Workers must be trained to interact safely with robots, understand their limitations, and manage emergencies or anomalies. Training should include not only programming and maintaining robots but also monitoring their operations and ensuring compliance with safety regulations. This transition requires a significant shift in workers' professional profiles, adapting to new roles and responsibilities in an automated work environment.

Cybersecurity is another critical implication of advanced robotics. With the rise of networked autonomous robots and software-controlled systems, the risk of cyberattacks compromising worker safety increases. A cyberattack on a robotic system could result in dangerous malfunctions, with potentially disastrous consequences in industrial or high-risk environments. Robotic systems must be protected not only against physical risks but also against digital threats by implementing cybersecurity protocols such as multi-factor authentication, encrypted communications, and network segregation.

The psychological impact of advanced robotics on workers must also be considered. Concerns about job displacement are a recurring theme in automation discussions, and integrating robotics may generate uncertainty and anxiety among employees. While robots can improve physical safety, they may also create a work environment where individuals feel pressured or insecure about their roles. Companies must address these concerns by providing adequate information and training on robotics' benefits and workers' continued roles in an increasingly automated workplace.

Safety regulations are a central element in managing the implications of advanced robotics on worker safety. Current European regulations, such as the Machinery Directive, require robot manufacturers and users to ensure devices comply with strict safety standards. With the advent of advanced technologies, regulations are likely to be updated to address specific risks related to human-robot interaction, cybersecurity, and AI algorithm use in industrial robots. Companies must be aware of these regulations and ensure compliance through regular audits and adopting best safety practices.

How can the Internet of Things improve safety on construction sites?

The Internet of Things is significantly transforming safety on construction sites, offering new opportunities to monitor the work environment, prevent accidents, and enhance real-time safety management. In construction sites, traditionally exposed to numerous physical and operational risks, the use of sensors, connected devices, and data analysis platforms enables smart solutions that not only reduce hazards but also improve overall operational efficiency.

A fundamental aspect is real-time hazard detection. With IoT sensors, it's possible to continuously monitor the environmental conditions of construction sites, detecting excessive temperatures, noise levels beyond safety thresholds, toxic gasses, or hazardous dust. Sensors can also detect if a worker is in an area not designated for their tasks, is not wearing personal protective equipment (PPE), or is not using safety equipment or fall prevention systems correctly. Strategically placed sensors can transmit real-time alerts to safety managers when abnormal data is detected. For instance, if a sensor identifies the presence of dangerous gasses like carbon monoxide, an alarm can immediately notify workers and supervisors, enabling evacuation and the activation of necessary safety procedures.

IoT also enhances individual worker safety through smart wearable devices. These devices, such as helmets or vests equipped with sensors, can continuously monitor workers' physical conditions, detecting signs of fatigue, heat stress, dehydration, or other issues that might compromise safety. Additionally, wearables can include geolocation features to track workers' positions on-site and enable rapid intervention during emergencies. For example, if a worker strays from a safe area or enters a hazardous zone, the system can send a warning to the safety officer or the worker themselves, thereby reducing the risk of accidents.

Another critical use of IoT in construction sites is monitoring machinery and equipment. Sensors attached to machinery can continuously track their operational status, detecting anomalies, imminent failures, or unsafe usage conditions. Predictive maintenance allows for intervention before a failure occurs, reducing the risk of accidents caused by sudden malfunctions. Furthermore, real-time monitoring of heavy equipment, such as cranes or excavators, can prevent operational errors or misuse, improving overall site safety.

IoT also facilitates better emergency management on construction sites. In case of an incident or emergency, IoT devices can automatically activate evacuation procedures, send notifications to all personnel, and coordinate rescue efforts. For example, in the event of a collapse or fire, sensors can immediately detect the situation and trigger automated alarms. Wearable location devices also allow responders to pinpoint the exact positions of workers, enabling quick interventions to ensure their safety. This type of automated coordination significantly improves emergency response and reduces intervention times, which are crucial for mitigating incident consequences.

Another significant advantage of IoT in construction sites is improved management of access to critical areas. Sensors and connected devices can control access to specific zones, authorizing only personnel with the necessary skills or equipment to operate there. On sites with hazardous materials or high-risk operations, IoT can verify workers' identities through badges or wearable identification devices and grant access only to those who have completed required training or are equipped with appropriate PPE. This automated control reduces the risk of unauthorized or unprepared individuals entering dangerous areas, enhancing overall site safety.

Lastly, IoT can be used to improve worker training and awareness regarding safety. By collecting and analyzing data related to site safety, IoT platforms can identify recurring risk areas or unsafe worker behaviors. These data can be used to adapt and enhance safety training programs, raising awareness of potential hazards and best practices for avoiding them. The collected data can also generate detailed reports on incidents or near-misses, facilitating root cause analysis and the implementation of corrective measures.

What are the challenges to physical safety in digitized workplaces?

Digitized workplaces offer numerous opportunities to enhance efficiency and productivity, but they also introduce new challenges in terms of physical safety. Digitalization, through technologies such as automation, artificial intelligence, IoT, and advanced robotics, fundamentally changes the work environment and how workers interact with equipment and systems. Consequently, new vulnerabilities arise that require updated approaches to ensure worker safety.

One primary issue involves human-machine interaction. The introduction of autonomous and collaborative robots in factories, warehouses, and construction sites leads to increasingly close interactions between workers and advanced machinery. While cobots are designed to work alongside humans, there remains a risk of collisions, programming errors, or malfunctions that could endanger people. Ensuring safety in such scenarios requires advanced sensor systems and detection technologies that can immediately halt robot operations in case of danger, as well as continuous worker training on safe interactions with these machines.

Another significant challenge is the cybersecurity of physical systems. In digitized workplaces, many physical devices are connected to networks via IoT, creating new attack surfaces for cybercriminals. These attackers may target machinery control systems or safety sensors to cause malfunctions, operational disruptions, or even physical accidents. A cyberattack compromising an automated machine's functionality could result in dangerous failures, putting workers' lives at risk. Protecting these systems requires robust cybersecurity measures, including isolated networks, data encryption, and strict access controls to ensure that only authorized personnel can interact with critical systems.

Wearable technologies and smart devices are increasingly common in digitized workplaces, but these solutions also present challenges. Smart wearables, such as helmets or vests with sensors, are used to monitor workers' health and safety, detecting parameters such as heart rate, body temperature, or exposure to hazardous substances. However, these devices must operate reliably in challenging conditions, and if poorly designed or if the data they collect is not properly managed, they might fail when most needed. Additionally, reliance on digital data could lead to situations where connectivity issues or device malfunctions compromise safety.

The operational complexity of digitized systems is another critical factor. Workers must manage and maintain a variety of complex machinery, requiring thorough and ongoing training. Errors in using digital systems, either due to insufficient understanding of the technology or inadequate training, can lead to accidents. Furthermore, the rapid evolution of advanced technologies may force workers to quickly learn how to use new systems, increasing the risk of errors.

Emergency management in a digitalized context also presents vulnerabilities, such as potential IT failures or power outages that could compromise system effectiveness. Organizations must ensure manual backup plans and train workers to respond effectively even without digital support.

Lastly, the psychological implications of digitalization on workers' well-being should not be overlooked. Increased automation and artificial intelligence can lead to significant changes in job roles, causing uncertainty or anxiety about job security. This type of psychological stress can affect concentration and performance, indirectly increasing accident risk. Companies must address these challenges by clearly communicating changes, providing support, and training workers to feel comfortable in new digital environments.

How can real-time data be used to improve worker safety?

The use of real-time data is one of the most effective strategies to enhance worker safety in industrial, construction, and other high-risk activities. Current technologies enable continuous monitoring of the work environment, equipment conditions, and workers' physical status. Access to real-time data allows for the timely detection of hazardous situations and intervention before accidents occur, thereby improving prevention and protection.

One key advantage of real-time data is the ability to continuously monitor environmental conditions. Distributed sensors can collect data on various critical parameters such as temperature, humidity, air quality, noise levels, and the presence of toxic gases. In industries like chemicals or construction, workers may be exposed to rapidly changing conditions that, if unmonitored, can jeopardize their health. Real-time data enables supervisors to receive automatic alerts when exposure levels to hazardous substances exceed safety thresholds, facilitating immediate intervention, evacuation of the area, or activation of ventilation systems.

Smart wearable devices are another essential tool that leverages real-time data to enhance worker safety. Devices such as bracelets, helmets, or vests with integrated sensors can continuously monitor workers' vital parameters and their interactions with the operational environment, helping to prevent accidents caused by physical conditions that could compromise safety.

Real-time data can also be utilized to monitor and maintain equipment and machinery. Sensors installed on heavy or complex machinery can detect operational anomalies, such as excessive vibrations, component wear, or overheating.

This information enables predictive maintenance, preventing sudden failures that could cause accidents or endanger workers. If a sensor detects that a machine is operating outside safe parameters, the system can trigger an alert signaling the need for immediate intervention or automatically shut down the machine to prevent damage.

Another important application of real-time data is risk management and collision prevention. In construction sites, factories, or warehouses, workers often operate near industrial vehicles or moving machinery such as cranes or forklifts. Proximity sensors and geolocation systems can track the movements of workers and machinery, automatically flagging situations where collision risks exist. These systems can warn both the worker and the machine operator of potential hazards or trigger an automatic stop if excessive proximity is detected.

Real-time data also improves emergency management. In case of an incident, connected sensors and devices can activate alarms and send information to safety managers. Location devices allow for the precise tracking of workers within the work area, facilitating rescue and evacuation operations. Additionally, real-time monitoring systems can collect data on surrounding conditions, such as smoke spread or the presence of toxic substances, and provide this information to first responders, enabling more effective and safer interventions, and guiding decisions on prioritizing necessary actions.

What are the safety requirements for wearable devices used by workers?

Wearable devices used by workers are a significant innovation for improving workplace safety. To ensure these devices provide real benefits without introducing new risks, it is essential to comply with safety requirements.

The first requirement is data protection and privacy. Since many wearable devices monitor real-time physical and environmental parameters, collecting sensitive worker data, it is critical to protect this data from unauthorized access. This includes the use of encryption to secure data transmitted from the device to centralized management systems, as well as security measures to ensure only authorized personnel can access the collected data. In Europe, wearable devices must comply with the General Data Protection Regulation (GDPR).

Another important requirement is the robustness and durability of the device. Wearables must be designed to withstand the challenging conditions of many work environments, such as extreme temperatures, exposure to dust, vibrations, or chemicals. They must be constructed with durable materials that do not degrade easily and that do not pose risks to the worker. For example, a smart vest used on a construction site must be able to endure daily wear without breaking or losing functionality.

Compliance with safety standards and regulations is another essential requirement for wearable devices. These devices must adhere to local, national, and international occupational safety regulations. In Europe, personal protective equipment such as helmets, vests, and safety shoes must comply with Directive 89/686/EEC and Regulation (EU) 2016/425, which establish minimum requirements for the design, manufacturing, and use of PPE. Wearable devices with technological functionalities must also meet specific standards for electronics and IoT devices, as set by regulations on electromagnetic compatibility and electrical safety.

Ergonomics and comfort are also critical for wearable devices. Since workers must wear these devices for long periods, they must be ergonomically designed and should not interfere with daily work activities. A device that is too heavy, bulky, or uncomfortable could distract the worker or restrict movement, increasing the risk of accidents. Manufacturers must ensure that the devices are lightweight, easy to wear, and adaptable to the body, so they do not compromise mobility or comfort.

The functional safety of the device is another essential requirement. Wearables must be designed to be reliable and to avoid malfunctions that could endanger workers. For instance, a smart helmet monitoring exposure to harmful gasses must reliably alert the worker in case of danger. In critical environments where safety depends on the device's proper functioning, it is essential for wearables to have self-diagnosis functions and failure alarms. For this reason, they must undergo rigorous testing to verify their reliability under real working conditions.

Another important requirement is usability and intuitive interface design. Wearable devices must be simple to use and should not require complex training. The user interface should be designed to provide clear and easily understandable information, avoiding cognitive overload for the worker. This means that if a wearable emits safety alerts, they must be easily recognizable and understandable, even in stressful or emergency situations.

Wearable devices used by workers must also be easy to maintain and update, particularly if equipped with software or connected to IoT networks. Manufacturers should provide regular updates to address potential security vulnerabilities or improve functionalities. Periodic checks should also be conducted to ensure the devices are functioning correctly and remain compliant with safety standards. Easy maintenance is critical to ensuring the device's longevity and effectiveness.

Lastly, compatibility with other safety and management systems is an important requirement for wearable devices. Since many devices are connected to centralized safety management platforms or company networks, they must be compatible with other systems used in the organization, such as emergency management software, access control systems, or environmental monitoring devices. The ability to integrate data collected by wearables with other safety tools provides a comprehensive view of working conditions and facilitates proactive safety management.

How can augmented reality technologies contribute to workplace safety training?

Augmented reality (AR) technologies are emerging as powerful tools for workplace safety training, offering an immersive and interactive way to learn and practice safety measures in controlled and simulated environments. Unlike traditional training methods that rely on manuals, videos, or lectures, AR allows workers to interact with realistic simulations of their work environment, enabling them to develop practical skills and a deeper awareness of risks in a safe and effective manner.

One major advantage of AR is the ability to simulate realistic risk scenarios, helping workers understand the hazards associated with their jobs and learn how to respond correctly in emergencies. Using headsets or mobile devices, workers can visualize hazardous situations, such as gas leaks, fires, collapses, or mechanical failures, and practice safety procedures in a safe, risk-free setting. For example, a construction worker could use AR to simulate working on an unstable scaffold, learning how to stabilize it and adopt proper personal protective measures.

AR also offers the ability to provide real-time instructions during work operations, enhancing situational safety awareness. For instance, a worker wearing AR glasses could receive visual overlays showing step-by-step instructions or warnings directly in their field of view, guiding them through correct procedures or alerting them to hidden dangers. This type of real-time support significantly improves safety in high-risk tasks, such as assembling complex machinery, maintaining industrial equipment, or operating heavy tools. By eliminating the need to consult manuals or printed instructions during tasks, workers can fully concentrate on their activities without distractions.

AR technologies can also be used to monitor trainees' performance and provide immediate, personalized feedback. During a simulated fire evacuation, for instance, the AR system could track a worker's movements, assessing their responsiveness and effectiveness in following safety procedures. If the worker makes an error—such as choosing an incorrect escape route or failing to activate an alarm—the AR system can provide real-time corrections, helping the trainee understand their mistake and improve their performance. This interactive and tailored training approach is far more effective than traditional methods, allowing workers to actively learn and receive specific feedback on their actions.

Another way AR supports safety training is through its ability to tailor learning to different levels of experience. Beginners can start with basic simulations that introduce fundamental safety concepts, while experienced workers can engage in more complex and role-specific scenarios. For example, a maintenance technician familiar with safety protocols could use AR to simulate repairing a machine in a high-risk area, considering factors such as chemical exposure or high-pressure systems. This modular approach enables training programs to be customized based on individual skills and needs, enhancing learning effectiveness.

AR also facilitates collaborative and team-based training in complex work environments. In industries like logistics or construction, where coordination among team members is critical for safety, AR can simulate collaborative operations, allowing workers to practice coordinating activities and managing emergencies virtually. Team members can be immersed in the same AR scenario, interact with each other, make joint decisions, and learn how to work together to resolve critical situations. This training improves communication and teamwork, essential elements for preventing workplace accidents.

Finally, AR can be used to provide continuous and updated training that adapts to changes in safety regulations or the introduction of new equipment or procedures. If a new machine is introduced in an industrial plant, workers can use AR to quickly learn how to operate it safely, viewing operational instructions and safety measures directly overlaid on the machine itself. This makes safety training an ongoing process that can be easily updated and improved, ensuring workers are always informed about best practices and the latest regulations.

What are the safety measures to prevent the misuse of autonomous machines?

Autonomous machines are becoming increasingly common across industries, improving efficiency and reducing human workloads. However, misuse of these technologies can pose significant risks to worker safety and infrastructure. To mitigate these risks, it is essential to implement effective safety measures that ensure the proper use of autonomous machines and minimize the potential for accidents or malfunctions.

One of the most critical safety measures is the implementation of advanced control and monitoring systems. Autonomous machines must be equipped with systems that continuously monitor their operations, detecting anomalies or suspicious behaviors. These systems can use artificial intelligence algorithms to identify operational errors, mechanical failures, or deviations from normal functioning parameters. If a potential risk is detected, the system can automatically halt the machine's operation and alert supervisors. This prevents human or technical errors from leading to the misuse of the machine and potential incidents.

Another essential aspect is access management. Only qualified and authorized personnel should have access to and control of autonomous machines. This can be ensured through robust authentication systems, such as biometric credentials, electronic identification cards, or unique access codes for each operator. By limiting machine access to trained individuals, the risk of misuse by unqualified personnel is significantly reduced. Additionally, access should be logged, recording who used the machine, when, and for how long, enabling continuous oversight and rapid identification of any improper use.

Autonomous machines must also be equipped with advanced safety sensors to monitor their surroundings and detect obstacles or hazards. Proximity sensors, 360-degree cameras, and radar can identify the presence of people, vehicles, or other objects near the machine, reducing the risk of collisions or other accidents. If a sensor detects an imminent danger, the system can automatically trigger an emergency stop or alter the machine's path.

Another fundamental safety measure is the implementation of emergency shutdown systems (kill switches) that allow operators to immediately stop an autonomous machine in case of an emergency or misuse. The emergency shutdown can be manually activated by the operator or automatically triggered by the machine's control system in the event of a malfunction or abnormal behavior. It is essential that these systems are easy to use and accessible at all times, enabling workers to intervene quickly if necessary.

Ongoing worker training is another crucial element in preventing the misuse of autonomous machines. Operators must receive adequate training not only on the correct use of machines but also on the associated risks and safety procedures to follow in emergencies. Training should be updated regularly to reflect technological advancements and new safety regulations. Additionally, fostering a safety culture encourages workers to promptly report any issues or risks related to the use of autonomous machines.

Regulations and safety certifications are also essential tools for ensuring the proper use of autonomous machines. In Europe, machines such as industrial robots must comply with the Machinery Directive and ISO 10218 standards, which establish safety requirements for industrial robots and their integration systems. These regulations mandate that autonomous machines be designed with inherent safety features, such as speed limitations, force control, and the ability to detect anomalies. Companies must ensure that all autonomous machines in use are certified, comply with these regulations, and undergo regular inspections to verify adherence to safety standards.

Finally, before deploying an autonomous machine in a real work environment, it is crucial to test it in a simulated setting to verify its ability to respond appropriately to emergencies or unexpected conditions. Rigorous testing can identify potential vulnerabilities or malfunctions and address them before the machine enters daily operational cycles. Simulations also help train operators, allowing them to learn how to manage the machine safely without real risks.

5. WORKERS' RIGHTS AND NEW TECHNOLOGIES

How can new technologies improve employees' working conditions?

New technologies hold the potential to significantly enhance employees' working conditions, providing tools that not only boost productivity but also promote well-being, safety, and quality of work life. From automation to process digitalization, artificial intelligence, and wearable devices, their application can positively impact various aspects of work by reducing physical and mental burdens, improving communication, and offering greater flexibility.

One primary way new technologies enhance working conditions is by reducing physical and repetitive labor. The introduction of robots and automated machinery in sectors such as manufacturing, logistics, and construction enables workers to avoid physically demanding tasks, thereby lowering the risk of musculoskeletal injuries or fatigue. For instance, the use of exoskeletons in factories allows employees to lift and carry heavy objects without straining their backs or joints, while collaborative robots can handle repetitive tasks, freeing workers to focus on higher-value activities. This reduction in physical workload not only improves health and safety but also reduces absenteeism and increases job satisfaction.

Another positive aspect is the improvement in communication and collaboration among employees through digital technologies. Advanced communication tools, such as online collaboration platforms, project management software, and video conferencing systems, allow workers to connect easily, regardless of their geographical location. This is particularly relevant in the context of remote or hybrid work, which has grown significantly in recent years. The ability to communicate quickly and efficiently facilitates information sharing, teamwork, and problem resolution. Additionally, collaborative platforms reduce the need for in-person meetings, providing employees with more flexible time management and improving work-life balance.

New technologies also provide tools to improve workplace safety. As previously mentioned, wearable devices such as smart vests, helmets, or glasses can monitor workers' physical conditions and their surroundings, detecting hazards and sending real-time alerts. These devices can prevent accidents and improve emergency response, protecting employees' health and safety. Furthermore, using artificial intelligence and data analysis for predictive maintenance of equipment helps prevent sudden breakdowns that could endanger workers. These technologies enhance not only physical safety but also employees' sense of security and well-being, as they feel more protected in their work environment.

Workplace flexibility is another significant benefit offered by new technologies. Remote work, enabled by high-speed internet, video conferencing software, and cloud collaboration tools, allows employees to work from anywhere, reducing the need for daily commutes. This increased flexibility positively impacts workers' psychological well-being by reducing stress related to commuting and providing more time for family and personal life. The result is that organizations adopting flexible work policies often experience increased productivity and higher employee satisfaction.

The automation of administrative and bureaucratic processes is another way in which new technologies improve working conditions. Using management software, artificial intelligence, and automation tools, many routine administrative tasks, such as payroll management, attendance tracking, or employee benefits administration, can be automated, reducing employees' workload and enabling them to focus on more strategic and creative tasks. This not only reduces stress related to bureaucratic activities but also makes work more rewarding and stimulating.

Advanced technologies can also enhance talent and human resource management within organizations. AI-driven tools can analyze employee performance data, identify development and training opportunities, and optimize career management. Employees can receive more accurate and personalized feedback as well as professional development plans tailored to their skills and aspirations. This approach can increase employee motivation and engagement while helping companies retain talent and foster a culture of growth and continuous improvement.

Finally, the use of green technologies, such as renewable energy and low-impact production processes, helps reduce an organization's ecological footprint, creating a healthier and more sustainable work environment for employees. Workers who perceive their employer as committed to sustainability are often more motivated and engaged, as they view their contributions as part of a broader organizational commitment to the greater good.

What are workers' rights regarding the use of personal data in the workplace?

Workers' rights regarding the use of personal data in the workplace are governed by regulations aimed at protecting two key aspects: privacy and personal dignity. In Europe, the GDPR (General Data Protection Regulation) is the primary legislative framework that establishes workers' rights concerning personal data processing. These rights apply to any information that can identify a person, including personal data, health information, behavioral data, and information collected through surveillance or performance monitoring systems.

One of the primary rights recognized by the GDPR is the right to information. Workers must be clearly and transparently informed about what personal data their employer collects, how it is used, for what purposes, and with whom it may be shared. This information must be provided in an easily understandable and accessible format, such as a privacy notice and a company policy on data processing. The employer must also indicate the legal basis for data processing, such as the worker's consent, compliance with legal obligations, the necessity of processing data to perform a contract, or the protection of vital interests of the individual—such as data collected for health and safety systems.

Another fundamental right is the right of access. Workers have the right to know whether their employer is processing their personal data and, if so, to obtain a copy of the data. This includes information about the purpose of the processing, the categories of data processed, the recipients of the data, and the expected retention period. Workers can request this information at any time, and employers must respond within a reasonable timeframe. The right of access ensures transparency and allows workers to verify that their data is being processed lawfully.

The right to rectification is another crucial aspect for workers. If an employee finds that their personal data is incorrect, incomplete, or outdated, they have the right to request immediate correction. The employer is obligated to rectify or supplement inaccurate or incomplete data. This right is fundamental to ensuring that the processed information is accurate and accurately reflects the worker's situation, particularly for purposes such as attendance management, performance evaluations, or payroll data.

A related right is the right to erasure, also known as the "right to be forgotten." Workers can request the deletion of their personal data under certain circumstances, such as when the data is no longer necessary for the purposes for which it was collected or when the worker withdraws their previously given consent. However, the right to erasure is not absolute, as employers may be required to retain some data to comply with legal or contractual obligations, such as keeping tax documents or payroll records.

The right to restrict processing allows workers to request limited use of their personal data in certain cases, such as when they dispute the accuracy of the data or when the data collected exceeds the permissible purposes. During the restriction period, the employer can store the data but cannot actively use it.

The right to data portability enables workers to receive their personal data in a structured, commonly used, and machine-readable format, as well as to transfer it to another data controller. This right is primarily applicable when data processing is based on the worker's consent or a contract and can be useful when changing jobs or transferring information between employers.

Workers also have the right to object to the processing of their personal data in certain circumstances. If data processing is based on the employer's legitimate operational needs or obligations, workers can object. However, the employer may demonstrate compelling legitimate grounds to continue processing the data, overriding the worker's rights and freedoms. Under broader labor regulations, workers can object to continuous monitoring of their activities, particularly if it infringes on their privacy.

Monitoring and electronic surveillance in the workplace is a prominent issue in modern work environments. If employers use monitoring tools, such as surveillance cameras, computer usage tracking software, or location-tracking systems, they must comply with GDPR principles, including data minimization, transparency, and proportionality. Workers must be informed about the existence and purpose of such systems, while employers must ensure monitoring is strictly limited to what is necessary for legitimate purposes, such as physical security and asset protection.

Finally, workers have the right not to be subjected to automated decisions (including profiling) that produce legal effects or significantly impact them without their consent or adequate human review. For example, if an employer uses an algorithm to evaluate employee performance or make career development decisions, the worker has the right to request a human review of the decision and express their perspective on the matter.

How will automation affect workers' rights in the manufacturing sector?

Automation in the manufacturing sector is rapidly transforming the way factories and production lines operate, introducing technologies such as collaborative robots, automated machinery, and artificial intelligence systems. This shift will significantly impact workers' rights, affecting various aspects of their employment, including safety, required skills, career opportunities, and protection against technological unemployment.

One of the most apparent impacts of automation relates to the right to workplace safety. Automation has the potential to significantly improve worker safety in manufacturing by reducing exposure to hazardous and strenuous tasks. Robots can be programmed to perform repetitive and risky operations, such as lifting heavy loads or handling dangerous materials, allowing workers to focus on less physically demanding and safer activities. However, integrating autonomous robots and complex machinery also requires workers to be adequately trained to understand the risks of interacting with these technologies. The right to adequate and continuous training ensures that workers can operate safely alongside automated systems.

Another significant consequence of automation concerns the right to employment. The introduction of automated systems may reduce the demand for unskilled labor, as many manual tasks traditionally performed by workers can be executed more efficiently by machines. This poses a risk of technological unemployment, especially for less-skilled workers. To address this issue, workers need protection through policies promoting reskilling (professional retraining) and upskilling (enhancing existing skills) that enable them to acquire new abilities required in an automated workplace. The right to continuous training will thus become essential to help workers adapt to technological changes and maintain employability.

Automation may also impact the right to fair remuneration. While automation can reduce labor demand, it can simultaneously increase productivity and improve corporate profits. In this context, workers could claim their right to share in these gains through salary increases or productivity-related incentives. It is vital to ensure that these benefits are equitably distributed, avoiding a growing disparity between highly skilled workers, who oversee machines, and less-skilled workers, whose roles may be progressively reduced or eliminated.

Automation raises concerns regarding monitoring and personal data protection. With the introduction of smart machines and IoT sensors, production processes are subject to increasingly detailed continuous monitoring, including real-time data collection. Directly or indirectly, such systems can gather data on workers' performance and behavior in the workplace. Workers must retain their right to privacy, ensuring that any collection of personal data complies with data protection regulations. They must be informed about what data is collected, how it is used, and for how long it will be retained, as well as have the option to oppose unnecessary or invasive data processing.

Another impact of automation pertains to the right to collective bargaining. As automation may drastically alter employment structures within a company—shifting demand toward technical skills and decreasing manual jobs—it will likely necessitate revisions to existing contractual agreements. Unions and workers' organizations will play a critical role in ensuring that automation does not lead to a reduction in rights or working conditions and in negotiating new contracts that reflect the realities of automated labor. They must ensure the protection of wages, safety conditions, and reskilling opportunities for workers whose roles are automated.

Automation could also influence the right to a fair working schedule. Increased operational efficiency through automation could reduce the need for long or excessive shifts, creating opportunities to shorten the workweek or increase workers' leisure time. In some cases, unions have already begun exploring contracts that provide for shorter workweeks without reducing pay, aligning with productivity gains achieved through automation. However, it is crucial to implement such changes equitably, avoiding increased pressure on remaining workers to complete more tasks in less time.

As new roles and areas of expertise emerge, automation could ultimately create new opportunities for workers. If managed appropriately, it could shift focus from repetitive manual tasks to more creative, analytical, and supervisory responsibilities, enhancing job quality and opening new career prospects. The right to a dignified and fulfilling career could be strengthened, provided workers are given the necessary tools to navigate the technological transition.

What training opportunities do new technologies offer workers?

New technologies are revolutionizing how workers acquire new skills and advance their careers, offering a wide range of training opportunities. Tools such as artificial intelligence, virtual reality, e-learning platforms, and automated learning systems have made training more accessible, customizable, and effective compared to traditional methods.

For years, new technologies have enabled remote learning or e-learning. Online learning platforms allow workers to access courses and training materials anytime, anywhere, overcoming the time and location constraints of traditional classroom-based training. Through e-learning, workers can take courses on a wide range of topics, from technical and professional skills to time management and personal development. These platforms also offer significant flexibility, enabling workers to learn at their own pace, which is especially valuable for those balancing training with work and family responsibilities.

Artificial intelligence (AI) is now transforming training through personalized learning experiences. AI systems can create adaptive learning paths tailored to individual workers' specific needs. By analyzing a person's current skills, progress, and areas for improvement, AI can suggest targeted training content to address identified gaps. This personalized approach not only makes training more effective but also increases workers' motivation by enabling them to track tangible progress and receive timely feedback. Additionally, AI can be used to create interactive quizzes and tests, helping workers consolidate their knowledge and measure their advancement over time.

Technologies like virtual reality (VR) and augmented reality (AR) provide important training opportunities by creating immersive environments and realistic simulations. These tools allow workers to practice practical scenarios safely. For instance, in high-risk sectors like manufacturing, construction, or healthcare, workers can use VR to simulate emergency situations, such as a machine malfunction or a complex surgical procedure, learning how to manage them safely. AR, on the other hand, can provide real-time visual instructions during operations, such as maintaining machinery or assembling complex components, improving precision and worker competence.

New technologies are also facilitating collaborative learning and teamwork. Digital platforms enable workers to participate in group projects and collaborate with colleagues from different parts of the world. Through tools like video conferencing, corporate chat platforms, shared workspaces, and project management systems, employees can work together on common problems, exchange knowledge and skills, and learn from each other. This form of learning fosters the development of soft skills, such as communication, teamwork, and problem-solving, which are increasingly valued in today's work environments. It remains essential, however, to ensure that online interaction platforms preserve adequate space for interpersonal relationships, safeguarding opportunities for direct collaboration among colleagues in the workplace.

Gamification is another emerging trend in worker training. This approach uses game elements, such as points, leaderboards, and challenges, to make learning more engaging and motivating. Training platforms that incorporate gamification allow workers to earn points, achieve badges, or level up as they complete training modules. This makes learning less monotonous and more interactive, increasing employee participation. Moreover, gamification encourages positive competition, motivating participants to improve their performance.

Microlearning platforms represent another significant opportunity for worker training. Microlearning involves delivering training content in short, focused sessions—typically just a few minutes long—that can be easily integrated into the workday. Through brief videos, infographics, quizzes, or interactive modules, workers can quickly and effectively acquire new skills without disrupting daily activities. This format is particularly effective for learning specific skills and for the ongoing updating of knowledge.

New technologies also enable real-time monitoring and evaluation of training progress. Digital platforms allow employers to track employees' progress, assess their performance in tests and quizzes, and identify areas needing further training. This continuous monitoring capability makes it possible to further personalize training paths and ensure each worker receives the support and resources necessary to develop required skills. Additionally, workers can view their progress and set learning goals, increasing their motivation and sense of responsibility toward training.

In a rapidly evolving labor market where required skills change frequently, the ability to continue learning and updating oneself is crucial. Digital platforms make continuous training more accessible and flexible, enabling employees to acquire new skills as new technologies emerge or as new business processes are introduced. This helps workers remain competitive in the labor market and advance in their careers.

How can workers' privacy be ensured with the increasing use of IoT devices?

The growing use of IoT devices in workplaces offers numerous advantages in terms of efficiency, safety, and performance monitoring. However, this technology also raises concerns about workers' privacy, as sensors and connected devices can collect vast amounts of personal and professional data. Ensuring workers' privacy in this context requires a balanced approach that leverages responsible technology use while respecting employees' rights.

Firstly, it is essential for employers to adopt a transparency-based approach. Workers must be clearly informed about which IoT devices are being used, what personal or professional data is being collected, for what purposes, how this data is processed, and with whom it may be shared. Therefore, a detailed privacy notice, compliant with data protection regulations, is necessary. Transparency is crucial for building trust between employers and employees, who must always be fully aware of how their information is being collected and managed.

Another key aspect is informed consent. When data collected by IoT devices is not strictly necessary to comply with legal or contractual obligations—and in other cases defined by law where consent is not required—employers must obtain explicit consent from workers for data processing. Consent must be free, informed, and revocable at any time. Workers have the right to accept or refuse the collection of non-essential data without facing repercussions. For example, if an IoT device collects data about movement patterns or the use of spaces within the workplace, workers' consent is required since this information could affect their privacy.

Data minimization is a key principle to uphold workers' privacy. Employers must collect only the data strictly necessary to achieve legitimate purposes and avoid collecting unnecessary or invasive information. For example, if the purpose of an IoT device is to monitor workplace safety, the data collected should focus on safety-related aspects and not include irrelevant personal information, such as workers' exact location at all times or their personal interactions.

Another important measure to ensure privacy is the adoption of adequate technical and organizational measures to protect the data collected by IoT devices. This includes encrypting data during transmission and storage to ensure that workers' personal information is not accessible to unauthorized persons. Authentication and access control systems should be implemented to restrict data availability to those who genuinely need it for their duties. Employers must also ensure that IoT technology providers meet the same security standards and can guarantee data protection throughout the device's lifecycle.

The use of IoT devices should also be subject to a thorough data protection impact assessment, especially when it involves processing sensitive or large-scale data. The DPIA (Data Protection Impact Assessment) is a procedure that helps employers assess the privacy risks associated with IoT technologies and identify necessary measures to mitigate these risks. This assessment should be conducted before introducing new IoT devices into the workplace and updated periodically to ensure protective measures remain adequate.

Data retention limitation is another fundamental principle. Personal data collected by IoT devices must be stored only for as long as necessary to achieve the purposes for which it was collected. Once the purpose is fulfilled, the data must be deleted or anonymized so it cannot be used to identify workers in the future. For example, if an IoT device collects attendance data for security reasons, this data should be deleted as soon as it is no longer needed for site safety monitoring.

Another measure to protect workers' privacy is ensuring their rights as data subjects, as outlined in the GDPR or other relevant regulations, remain enforceable regardless of the technology enabling data processing. These include the right of access to personal data, the right to rectification, the right to erasure, the right to restrict processing, and the right to object to processing. Workers must be able to exercise these rights easily and without obstacles, and employers must respond to such requests promptly and within a reasonable time frame.

What are workers' rights regarding electronic surveillance in the workplace?

Workers' rights regarding electronic surveillance in the workplace are governed by regulations aimed at balancing employees' right to privacy with employers' legitimate need to monitor activities for purposes such as safety, property protection, or productivity. In Europe, the General Data Protection Regulation (GDPR) is the main legal framework regulating electronic surveillance and ensuring workers' rights. National labor laws may contain specific provisions on remote surveillance; however, as some of these regulations date back to earlier times, they may not fully reflect the capabilities of modern technology.

First, the right to information and transparency must be highlighted. Workers must be clearly informed if they are subject to electronic surveillance, whether through cameras, email monitoring, activity tracking, call recording, personal data collection via platforms, IoT networks, proximity or motion sensors, or wearable technology capable of recording and transmitting information on vital parameters. This information must be provided transparently and before implementing surveillance, typically through a detailed company policy that explains the purposes of the surveillance, the methods used, and the type of data collected. The GDPR also requires employers to inform workers about the legal basis justifying such surveillance, which may range from fulfilling contractual obligations to protecting the company's legitimate interests, provided these are balanced against employees' privacy rights.

Another fundamental right is the right to privacy. Even though employers may implement surveillance systems for legitimate reasons, they must respect workers' privacy boundaries. Surveillance must not be invasive beyond what is necessary and should be limited to what is proportionate to the declared purposes. For example, indiscriminately monitoring workers' private communications or using cameras in private areas like changing rooms or break rooms is not permitted. The principle of proportionality is key to ensuring that surveillance does not become an unjustified violation of workers' personal spheres.

Workers always have the right to access their personal data, regardless of the technological means used to collect it. If data is gathered through surveillance systems, videos, voice recordings, or tracking online activities, workers have the right to know what data has been collected, how it is processed, and how long it will be stored. They are also entitled to request a copy of the collected personal data. Employers must respond to access requests within a reasonable timeframe, usually one month, and provide this information in an understandable and accessible format.

Another important right is the ability to object to the processing of personal data through electronic surveillance, especially if such monitoring is based on the employer's legitimate interests. Workers can oppose surveillance if they believe it violates their privacy or if there are insufficient reasons to justify monitoring. If workers exercise this right, employers must demonstrate overriding legitimate grounds to continue surveillance that outweigh workers' rights and freedoms. Otherwise, the surveillance must cease.

The principle of data minimization is another key safeguard under the GDPR that applies to remote monitoring. In practice, employers may collect only the data necessary to achieve the specific purposes of surveillance and may not gather superfluous or irrelevant information. For example, if the goal of surveillance is to ensure the physical security of a building, camera monitoring should be limited to common areas where access occurs and should not include constant monitoring of personal spaces or individual workstations unless there are specific justified reasons.

Workers are also entitled to limit data processing. They may request temporary or continuous restrictions on the use of their data collected through electronic surveillance, for example, if they contest the accuracy of the data or believe the processing violates regulations. During the verification period, employers may retain the data but cannot actively use it to make decisions or for further processing unless necessary for legal or safety reasons.

Finally, workers have the right to erasure (the so-called "right to be forgotten"). If data collected through electronic surveillance is no longer necessary for the purposes for which it was gathered or has been processed unlawfully, workers can request its deletion. However, as with other rights, the right to erasure is not absolute and may be limited by legal obligations or legitimate business needs, such as retaining data for security purposes or contractual compliance.

How can artificial intelligence technologies support worker safety?

Artificial intelligence technologies are rapidly transforming workplace safety management, providing advanced tools to improve accident prevention, reduce risks, and actively protect workers. AI enables real-time analysis of large volumes of data, anomaly detection, and the prediction of potential hazards, contributing to a safer work environment.

One of the most significant uses of AI in workplace safety is through predictive analysis and accident prevention. AI can collect and analyze data from IoT sensors, wearable devices, and surveillance systems, identifying patterns and trends that may indicate imminent risks. For example, in industrial settings, sensors can monitor machinery conditions and operational parameters, while AI processes this data to detect signs of wear or malfunctions that could lead to accidents. This enables companies to perform predictive maintenance, preventing sudden breakdowns and reducing the risk of injuries.

Another way AI supports safety is through intelligent wearable devices. Helmets, bracelets, or vests equipped with sensors continuously monitor workers' physical parameters. AI processes this data in real-time to detect signs of fatigue, dehydration, or other conditions that might compromise worker safety. For instance, if a worker shows signs of excessive fatigue, AI can alert safety managers, suggesting a break or other interventions to prevent accidents caused by lapses in attention.

AI can also be used to enhance environmental safety by detecting hazardous conditions such as excessive exposure to chemicals, high noise levels, or the presence of toxic gases. Environmental sensors collect real-time data, which AI analyzes to identify potentially dangerous situations. Workers can then be immediately alerted to evacuate an area or take safety measures before an accident occurs. This continuous monitoring is particularly valuable in high-risk sectors like chemical or mining industries, where hazards can rapidly change and require immediate responses.

A significant advantage of AI is its ability to improve safety training. Using virtual reality (VR) and augmented reality (AR), AI can create realistic simulations of risk scenarios, allowing workers to practice responding to emergencies without being exposed to real dangers. For example, in construction, workers can simulate the collapse of scaffolding or handling hazardous materials, learning to react correctly under the guidance of an AI system. This immersive training not only raises awareness of risks but also helps identify and address gaps in preparation.

AI can also monitor and analyze worker behavior, helping to identify habits that could lead to accidents. In warehouses or production plants, AI-based monitoring systems can detect if a worker is not following safety procedures, such as using personal protective equipment or maintaining safe distances from machinery. In case of violations, the system can automatically send alerts or intervene directly, stopping machinery or halting dangerous activities.

AI can further improve emergency management. In cases of fires or collapses, AI can assist in coordinating rescue operations more efficiently. AI systems can analyze real-time conditions and identify the safest evacuation routes, taking into account worker locations and environmental factors. Additionally, wearable devices equipped with GPS can help locate individuals in distress and prioritize those needing assistance, making rescue efforts more targeted and effective. AI can also suggest optimal intervention procedures based on historical data and predictive models.

Another area where AI can have a positive impact is reducing stress and workload. By analyzing data on work rhythms and productivity, AI can identify situations where workers are subjected to excessive loads or prolonged stress. In such cases, AI can recommend changes to work shifts, task redistribution, or other measures to alleviate pressure on workers, improving their overall well-being and reducing risks associated with fatigue.

Finally, AI can be used to ensure compliance with safety regulations. Systems can monitor in real-time whether companies adhere to all safety standards and guidelines, flagging any non-compliance and suggesting corrective actions. For example, AI can track the use of personal protective equipment (PPE) or verify whether safety inspections are conducted regularly and correctly, helping maintain high safety standards and avoid penalties related to non-compliance.

What are the implications of new technologies on work flexibility?

New technologies are significantly impacting work flexibility, transforming how workers organize their time, interact with colleagues, and manage responsibilities. These technologies—

including digital platforms, remote collaboration tools, artificial intelligence, and automation—are reshaping the boundaries and forms of the traditional workplace. However, they also bring challenges in managing work, balancing personal and professional life, and protecting workers' rights.

One of the primary changes brought about by new technologies is the rise of remote work. Tools such as video conferencing, online collaboration platforms, and cloud computing allow employees to work from anywhere, eliminating the need for physical office presence. This has led to the widespread adoption of remote work, offering greater flexibility in both schedules and work locations. Workers can better manage their time, avoid long commutes, and achieve a healthier balance between work, family, and personal life. In this context, the concept of a physical office is becoming less relevant, and companies are adopting hybrid work models that combine in-office and remote work.

Digital technologies have also facilitated changes in work organization, increasing opportunities for freelancing or short-term contracts. Digital platforms, such as on-demand work apps or freelance marketplaces, enable workers to access flexible job opportunities, select specific projects, or take on temporary assignments, adapting their workload to their needs. While this approach offers freedom and autonomy, it raises concerns about job security, income stability, and worker rights, which are not always guaranteed in short-term contracts or freelance arrangements.

Another implication of new technologies for work dynamics relates to artificial intelligence and automation. AI can efficiently manage repetitive tasks, freeing workers from manual activities and allowing them to focus on more complex and strategic responsibilities. This not only boosts productivity but also provides workers with greater freedom in managing their time and responsibilities. For example, automated scheduling software can organize daily activities more efficiently, considering individual preferences and workloads, and enabling employees to work more flexibly.

New technologies are also transforming time management within companies. Digital collaboration tools allow workers to communicate and collaborate with colleagues and teams across different parts of the world, overcoming time zone or physical presence constraints. This has led to greater flexibility in working hours, allowing employees to organize their activities based on preferred schedules, provided they meet corporate deadlines and objectives. However, this flexibility can also lead to an unintended extension of working hours, as boundaries between work and personal life become less defined, creating risks of overworking or professional burnout.

Beyond these risks, the increasing flexibility introduced by technology brings critical elements to be carefully assessed. One significant concern is the monitoring and surveillance of remote workers. The use of technologies to track employee activities, such as time-tracking software or digital surveillance systems, may conflict with privacy and workers' rights. Companies must adopt a balanced and respectful approach, ensuring that any monitoring is transparent, proportionate, and compliant with data protection regulations.

How can worker data security be ensured in a digital workplace?

Ensuring the security of worker data in a digital workplace is one of the most pressing challenges for companies, especially given the increasing use of digital tools, remote work, and the growing volume of data collected and processed through interconnected platforms and devices. To protect the personal and sensitive data of workers, companies must adopt a combination of technical, organizational, and procedural measures in compliance with data protection regulations.

A transparent approach is fundamental to building employee trust and ensuring that data processing complies with applicable regulations. A company's data protection policy should outline the security measures in place to protect personal information and ensure that employees are aware of their rights regarding access, rectification, and data deletion.

An essential aspect of data security is the implementation of technical measures to protect against cyberattacks and breaches. These include encrypting data both in transit and at rest, using firewalls, intrusion prevention systems (IPS), and antivirus software. Encryption ensures that sensitive data is only readable by authorized users, reducing the risk of unauthorized access or data theft. Similarly, adopting multifactor authentication technologies is critical to ensuring that only authorized personnel can access company systems and data, preventing account compromise due to weak or stolen passwords.

Another critical element is managing physical and virtual access. Companies must implement strict access controls, ensuring that only employees who need specific information to perform their jobs can access it. Adopting a principle of least privilege minimizes the risk of exposing sensitive data to unauthorized individuals. Additionally, monitoring and logging all user activities on company systems—recording access and performed operations—helps identify suspicious behavior or breach attempts promptly.

Organizations must also provide training and awareness programs to ensure workers are conscious of data security threats and best practices for protecting personal information. Training should cover topics such as the importance of strong passwords, recognizing phishing scams, the proper use of company devices, and the significance of safeguarding sensitive information. Employees often serve as the first line of defense against data breaches, making it essential that they are adequately prepared to identify and respond to potential threats.

In a digital workplace, especially with the growing prevalence of remote work, securing the devices used by employees is crucial. Companies must ensure that employees use secure and updated devices with the latest security patches. They should also implement policies regulating the use of personal devices for work purposes (known as BYOD, Bring Your Own Device). Additionally, using virtual private networks (VPNs) enhances the security of remote communications, ensuring that data transmitted between employee devices and company servers is encrypted and protected from interception.

Another measure to ensure data security is limiting data retention. Workers' personal data should only be retained for the time strictly necessary to achieve the purposes for which it was collected. Once the data is no longer needed, it should be securely deleted or anonymized in compliance with data protection regulations. Companies should also implement regular backup policies to ensure data is not lost due to technical errors or cyberattacks.

Data protection impact assessments (DPIAs) are another essential tool for ensuring worker data security. DPIAs are mandatory when data processing may present high risks to workers' rights and freedoms. Through a DPIA, companies can identify risks associated with data processing and implement the necessary measures to mitigate these risks before processing begins.

Lastly, organizations must establish procedures for managing data breaches. Despite all preventive measures, security breaches may still occur. Companies must be prepared to respond quickly and effectively, implementing a breach response plan that includes promptly notifying relevant authorities and affected workers, as required by GDPR. Organizations must also conduct thorough investigations to identify the cause of the breach and implement corrective measures to prevent its recurrence.

What are the legal challenges related to the use of collaborative robots in workplaces?

The use of collaborative robots, or cobots, in the workplace is rapidly increasing due to their ability to operate safely and efficiently alongside human workers. However, this technological innovation raises several legal challenges that must be addressed to ensure their safe and compliant integration into work activities. These challenges particularly concern worker safety, liability in case of accidents, data protection, and the safeguarding of employee rights.

One of the most critical aspects is worker safety. Cobots are designed to interact directly with humans, sharing workspaces and often performing repetitive or physically demanding tasks. Although cobots are generally considered safe, there is a risk of accidents or injuries, especially if the robot is not correctly programmed or trained or if a malfunction occurs. European regulations, particularly the Machinery Directive, establish safety requirements for industrial machinery, including collaborative robots. However, with the introduction of new technologies, these regulations may need updates to address the specific challenges posed by human-robot collaboration. Companies must ensure that cobots comply with international safety standards such as ISO 10218 and ISO/TS 15066, which outline design and operational safety requirements for industrial and collaborative robots.

Another legal challenge is determining liability in the event of accidents. If a cobot causes injury to a worker, it can be difficult to establish responsibility: the robot's manufacturer, the company using it, or the programmer who configured the system? Liability issues are particularly complex because cobot behavior can be influenced by a combination of factors, including AI systems and human interactions. Companies must adopt clear policies on liability management and ensure that robots undergo regular maintenance, safety inspections, and usage according to the manufacturer's instructions. Liability for damages caused by robots could also be governed by the principle of "product liability," which obliges manufacturers to ensure their products are safe and defect-free.

Data protection is another significant legal issue. Cobots

often come equipped with sensors, cameras, and AI systems that collect data about worker activities, work environments, and interactions with other machines. This data may include personal information, such as employee performance or movements within the workplace, raising concerns about privacy and data protection. Companies using cobots must ensure that data collection and processing comply with legal requirements. This includes informing workers about data collection, obtaining their consent where necessary, and implementing appropriate technical measures to protect collected data from unauthorized access or security breaches.

The use of cobots also raises questions about workers' rights. One of the most discussed aspects is the potential impact of cobots on employment. Although cobots are designed to collaborate with humans, there is concern that their widespread adoption may lead to job reductions, particularly in sectors such as manufacturing or logistics, where repetitive tasks are common. Companies must address this issue transparently, involving unions and worker representatives in discussions about cobot implementation and ensuring employees are adequately trained to work alongside robots. In some cases, renegotiating collective labor agreements may be necessary to accommodate changes in how work tasks are performed and to protect workers' rights.

6. PRODUCTS, MACHINES, INSTALLATIONS

What safety requirements for machine design are modified by Regulation (EU) 2019/1020?

Regulation (EU) 2019/1020 establishes a set of safety requirements focusing on market surveillance and compliance for products sold within the European Union. Its primary aim is to strengthen control over products placed on the European market, enhancing the safety of consumers and operators, including workers using complex machines. The regulation complements and reinforces the existing Machinery Directive, which governs the safe design of industrial machines.

A central goal of the regulation is to bolster market surveillance. This requires competent authorities in EU Member States to coordinate product inspections, ensuring compliance with the safety requirements established by European law. Currently, machines must adhere to safety standards that, while based on a common framework, are implemented through national legislation, leading to potential inconsistencies. The regulation addresses this by providing a uniform rule directly applicable across all Member States. It promotes greater cooperation among national authorities to ensure consistent market oversight throughout the EU, reducing the risk of non-compliant machines entering the European market via less regulated national channels.

Another key requirement introduced by the regulation pertains to the responsibility of economic operators across the supply chain. This obligation extends not only to manufacturers but also to importers and distributors, who must ensure that the products they market comply with EU regulations. In cases of non-compliance or safety risks, economic operators are required to take corrective actions, such as withdrawing or recalling products from the market. Additionally, they must cooperate with authorities during inspections or verifications, providing all necessary information to demonstrate that the machines meet safety requirements.

The regulation also introduces the concept of access to digital data from machines, in line with technological advancements and the proliferation of connected systems and IoT devices. Beyond traditional mechanical safety requirements, manufacturers must ensure the security of digital systems integrated into machines. For instance, machines equipped with software or connected to networks must be safeguarded against potential cyberattacks, and data collected via IoT devices must be securely managed. This new requirement reflects the growing importance of cybersecurity in machinery safety.

Another aspect of the regulation is its focus on the compliance of products imported from non-EU countries. The regulation stipulates that importers are responsible for ensuring that products from third countries comply with EU regulations before being marketed. This is a crucial step in combating the distribution of unsafe or counterfeit machines from external markets. Importers must verify that external manufacturers have conducted all necessary checks and provided the required compliance documentation, starting with CE certification.

The regulation places significant emphasis on information and transparency. Manufacturers, importers, and distributors are obligated to provide clear and precise information about machine safety features and safe usage methods. This includes the requirement to supply detailed and easily comprehensible user manuals, outlining risks associated with machine use and measures to prevent them. The information must be provided in the language of the country where the product is marketed, ensuring workers can understand the safety instructions.

Another notable aspect of the regulation concerns sustainability and resource efficiency. While not strictly a safety requirement, the regulation encourages designing machines that are not only safe but also energy-efficient and environmentally friendly. This aligns with the European Union's commitment to sustainability and reducing the environmental impact of industrial products.

Lastly, the regulation introduces stricter measures for managing non-compliance. If a machine fails to meet safety requirements, authorities can mandate its withdrawal from the market or the implementation of corrective measures to ensure compliance. To this end, the regulation provides for severe penalties for economic operators who violate the rules, including punitive measures for serious or repeated violations.

How do European regulations ensure the safety of innovative products?

European regulations prioritize the safety of innovative products by balancing the need to foster technological innovation with the protection of consumers and workers. This involves a combination of regulations, directives, and technical standards that define the safety requirements and compliance processes for products entering the market.

The current Machinery Directive establishes essential health and safety requirements for machines used in industrial and workplace settings. Although this directive was initially developed for traditional machinery and is set to be replaced by Regulation (EU) 2023/1230 in January 2027, it currently applies to innovative products, including collaborative robots and automated devices. The directive mandates that every product be designed and constructed to ensure operator safety during use, maintenance, and disposal. This includes risk assessment, the integration of safety systems, and measures to minimize hazards associated with machine use. Furthermore, manufacturers must ensure that products comply with technical standards providing specific guidelines to guarantee the safety of innovative devices.

Another key element in ensuring the safety of innovative products is Regulation (EU) 2019/1020, which strengthens market surveillance across the European Union. As discussed earlier, the regulation aims to ensure that products entering the market comply with EU safety, health, and environmental standards. It imposes an obligation on economic operators (manufacturers, importers, and distributors) to verify compliance with safety requirements before commercialization. Additionally, market surveillance authorities are authorized to conduct inspections and controls to ensure innovative products meet regulatory requirements. In cases of non-compliance, authorities can mandate product withdrawal or recall, providing a high level of protection for consumers and workers.

Compliance with innovative products is further ensured through adopting harmonized technical standards, developed by European and international bodies such as CEN and ISO. These standards provide detailed technical specifications for designing and ensuring the safety of technological products. While adopting these standards is voluntary, products that comply with harmonized standards benefit from a presumption of conformity with EU regulations, facilitating market access. This system ensures that innovative products are designed in accordance with best practices in safety and technology, minimizing risks for users.

Data protection for innovative products, particularly those involving artificial intelligence, IoT devices, and digital platforms, must also be guaranteed. GDPR establishes strict rules to ensure that personal data collected and processed by innovative devices are adequately protected. This is particularly relevant for technological products that gather user information, such as wearables, health monitoring systems, or domestic robots. According to the European data protection regulation, manufacturers of these devices must ensure that personal data are processed transparently, securely, and for declared purposes. They must also obtain explicit user consent for data processing and adopt technical measures such as encryption and anonymization to protect data from unauthorized access or security breaches.

The Medical Devices Regulation (EU) 2017/745 is another critical regulation ensuring the safety of innovative products in healthcare. The regulation establishes safety requirements for medical devices, including those incorporating advanced technologies like artificial intelligence and remote monitoring systems. It mandates rigorous conformity assessments before marketing medical devices, including clinical tests and safety trials. Additionally, manufacturers are required to continuously monitor the performance of their devices post-market, collecting real-world usage data to identify any safety issues or defects.

Finally, European regulations promote safe innovation through incentives and support programs for developing new technologies, provided they meet high safety standards. For example, the Horizon Europe research and innovation program (2021–2027) supports projects that advance technological innovation while adhering to safety regulations. This integrated approach allows the European Union to maintain a high level of consumer and worker protection while fostering growth in the technology sector.

What are the compliance requirements for new products entering the European Union market?

One of the primary compliance requirements for new products entering the European Union market is the CE marking. This indicates conformity with applicable EU regulations and certifies that the product meets essential safety, health, and environmental protection standards set out in European directives and regulations. The CE marking is mandatory for a wide range of products, including machinery, electronic devices, toys, medical devices, and construction products. To obtain the CE marking, manufacturers must conduct a conformity assessment, which may include internal testing, applying harmonized technical standards, and in some cases, involving a notified body to verify the product's compliance. Once the product meets the conformity requirements, the manufacturer can affix the CE marking and issue an EU Declaration of Conformity, certifying compliance with applicable regulations.

Another fundamental requirement is risk assessment. Before placing a product on the market, manufacturers are obliged to conduct a comprehensive risk assessment associated with the product's use. This process involves identifying potential hazards to safety, health, or the environment and adopting preventive measures to eliminate or mitigate those risks. For instance, the Machinery Directive requires machinery to be designed and constructed to minimize risks during normal use, including risks related to maintenance, cleaning, and decommissioning. The risk assessment must be documented and retained as part of the product's technical documentation.

Regarding technical documentation, manufacturers must prepare detailed information for each product placed on the market, demonstrating compliance with applicable regulations. This documentation includes technical drawings, diagrams, test results, descriptions of the product's operation, and a risk assessment. It must be retained for at least 10 years after the product is placed on the market and made available to competent authorities upon request. For products imported into the EU, importers must ensure they have access to the technical documentation and verify that the product complies with EU regulations before distribution.

The Market Surveillance Regulation (EU) 2019/1020 introduces additional requirements to ensure products on the market are safe and compliant. The regulation strengthens oversight by market surveillance authorities, which can inspect products, verify compliance with safety requirements, and implement corrective measures in cases of non-compliance. Economic operators (manufacturers, importers, and distributors) are required to cooperate with surveillance authorities and provide all necessary information to demonstrate product compliance. In the event of violations, authorities can mandate product withdrawals or recalls and impose sanctions.

Another compliance requirement concerns traceability. Manufacturers must ensure products are identifiable and traceable to their origin. This includes the obligation to display the manufacturer's name and address, a product identification number, and, where applicable, the CE marking on the product or its packaging. Economic operators must also maintain records of supply and distribution chains, ensuring that products can be traced in the event of safety issues or recalls.

In the context of medical devices, Regulation (EU) 2017/745 introduces specific requirements to ensure the safety and compliance of such products, including mandatory clinical evaluations, post-market surveillance, and reporting of incidents or defects. Medical devices must undergo rigorous safety and efficacy testing before being marketed, and manufacturers are required to continuously monitor device performance after commercialization to identify potential issues and implement corrective actions.

For innovative products involving digital technologies for collecting personal data, such as IoT devices or AI-based software, the GDPR imposes additional compliance requirements. Manufacturers must ensure that personal data collected by their products is processed in accordance with data protection regulations and that adequate technical and organizational measures are in place to safeguard user privacy. This includes adopting privacy-by-design and privacy-by-default principles, implementing data encryption and anonymization, and securely managing data throughout the product's lifecycle.

How do emerging technologies affect the regulation of industrial products?

Emerging technologies significantly impact the regulation of industrial products, necessitating constant updates to existing frameworks to ensure these innovations are safe, compliant, and beneficial for the market and society. Technologies like artificial intelligence (AI), the Internet of Things (IoT), advanced robotics, and blockchain are transforming not only production processes but also the nature of products themselves. Regulators must address new challenges to ensure that laws keep pace with technological evolution without hindering innovation.

A primary effect of emerging technologies is the need to adapt safety requirements. Industrial products incorporating new technologies, such as intelligent machinery or IoT devices, present different characteristics and risks compared to traditional products. For example, the introduction of collaborative robots (cobots) working alongside humans on production lines raises new safety concerns for workers. Regulators must update existing frameworks to address specific risks, such as preventing accidents arising from human-machine interaction. Current regulations must also be revised to include safety requirements that account for the decision-making autonomy of certain machines and AI-based systems. Harmonized technical standards are similarly subject to updates to include specific safety standards for products incorporating emerging technologies.

The growing use of innovative software in industrial products also requires regulators to address new issues related to liability. Traditionally, responsibility for defective industrial products rests primarily with manufacturers. However, with AI-based technologies, identifying liability becomes more complex. For instance, if an AI-equipped machine makes an error or causes an accident, determining whether responsibility lies with the machine manufacturer, the software developer, the system trainer, or the end-user can be challenging. This scenario calls for a revision of product liability laws and the establishment of new guidelines to define legal responsibility in complex cases involving autonomous or semi-autonomous technologies.

The rise of IoT introduces new regulatory challenges regarding cybersecurity. Connected industrial devices that collect and exchange real-time data can be vulnerable to cyberattacks.

Industrial product regulation must therefore include specific cybersecurity requirements to ensure IoT devices are protected against intrusions, malware, and other digital threats. The Cybersecurity Act (EU) 2019/881 represents an important step forward in harmonizing cybersecurity standards for connected products within the European Union. The regulation introduces a framework for certifying the security of IoT devices, but the rapid development of emerging technologies requires additional updates and specific rules to address new threats.

Emerging technologies like AI and blockchain also influence regulatory compliance and market surveillance methods. Regulatory authorities are exploring how these technologies can enhance their ability to monitor industrial products on the market and ensure compliance. For instance, blockchain can be used to create immutable records tracking a product's entire lifecycle, from manufacturing to distribution and disposal. This approach improves transparency and simplifies verifying product compliance with safety regulations and environmental directives. Additionally, authorities can use AI systems to analyze large datasets related to industrial products, identify patterns of non-compliance, and implement corrective measures more effectively and quickly.

Another area where emerging technologies impact regulation involves sustainability and environmental protection. Industrial products based on new technologies, such as electric vehicles or renewable energy devices, require specific regulations to ensure their contribution to the EU's sustainability goals, as outlined in the European Green Deal. For example, regulations on batteries and materials used in electric vehicles or energy storage systems must ensure they are safe, recyclable, and compliant with energy efficiency standards. IoT technologies can also play a role in the intelligent management of resources, helping reduce the environmental impact of industrial products. However, regulations must govern their use to ensure they do not lead to unintended negative effects, such as increased energy consumption or the generation of new electronic waste.

What are the safety requirements for new automated plants?

New automated plants represent a breakthrough in the industrial sector due to their ability to enhance productivity, efficiency, and operational precision. However, increased automation also introduces a series of safety concerns that must be addressed to ensure workers, the environment, and infrastructure are not exposed to risks. These issues are particularly relevant when emerging technologies are integrated into such plants.

One of the primary concerns involves the physical safety of workers interacting with automated machinery. In an automated plant, robots and machinery can perform operations autonomously or semi-autonomously, often sharing the same physical space with workers. This creates potential risks of collisions or accidents if safety measures are inadequate. To address this challenge, it is essential to implement safety devices such as presence detection sensors, safety barriers, and emergency stop systems to prevent incidents. Additionally, regulations like the Machinery Directive and international standards (e.g., ISO 10218 for industrial robots) mandate safety measures to minimize risks associated with automated machinery use.

Another critical issue is cybersecurity. Automated plants often use connected devices and integrate digital control systems that can be vulnerable to cyberattacks. An automated plant incorporating IoT technology, for example, can collect real-time data and communicate with other systems to optimize production processes. However, this interconnection introduces the risk of hackers accessing control systems, manipulating operations, or causing intentional damage to machinery. To mitigate this risk, plants must implement advanced cybersecurity measures, such as data encryption, firewalls, multifactor authentication, and continuous network monitoring. The Cybersecurity Act establishes a framework for certifying connected devices, including those used in automated plants, ensuring they meet specific security requirements.

Data management is another major challenge for the safety of automated plants. Machinery and automated systems generate and collect vast amounts of data related to operations, downtime, machinery conditions, and overall plant performance. While this data is crucial for optimizing production processes and improving efficiency, it must be handled carefully to prevent breaches or unauthorized access. Data loss or breaches could compromise plant safety or expose sensitive information. Automation systems must therefore be protected through data governance strategies that include regular backups, access controls, and data protection policies compliant with regulations such as the GDPR.

The complexity of systems also presents a challenge. Modern automated plants utilize a combination of advanced technologies, including sensors, actuators, robotics, and AI-driven software, which interact in complex ways to manage entire operational processes. Increased system complexity means a higher risk of malfunctions or programming errors that could jeopardize plant safety. For instance, an error in the control software could cause sudden production interruptions or, worse, damage machinery and endanger workers. To mitigate this risk, it is essential to subject systems to rigorous testing and implement preventive maintenance plans to ensure all components operate correctly.

Another safety issue for automated plants involves human-machine interaction. While many processes are automated, some operations still require human supervision or intervention. Managing interactions between workers and automated systems must be carefully planned to prevent human errors that could lead to accidents or malfunctions. Worker training becomes even more critical to ensure safe interactions with automated machinery and quick responses in emergencies. Additionally, the human-machine interface must be designed intuitively and provide clear, timely feedback to workers.

Finally, the operational resilience of automated plants is an emerging concern. With increased system complexity and connectivity, plants must withstand unexpected events such as power outages, hardware failures, or cyberattacks without compromising safety. This requires the implementation of business continuity plans and backup systems to ensure operations can resume quickly in case of failure. Integrating real-time monitoring and predictive diagnostics systems can help detect signs of potential problems before they become critical, enabling rapid and effective corrective measures.

How does Directive 2006/42/EC apply to new connected devices?

The Machinery Directive 2006/42/EC has been one of the EU's primary legislative tools for ensuring the safety of machinery used in industrial and workplace settings. Although the directive was drafted before the widespread adoption of IoT technologies and connected devices, it still applies to new industrial devices, including those incorporating connectivity technologies. However, technological evolution has raised new safety and compliance issues requiring a modern interpretation of the directive's requirements.

The Machinery Directive establishes essential health and safety requirements that every machine must meet before being placed on the market or put into service within the EU. These requirements cover the design, construction, and safe use of machinery, including control systems and moving parts. For connected devices, which may be linked to company networks or used in automated industrial environments, the directive mandates that these devices be designed to ensure safety not only for operators but also for anyone who may interact with the machine remotely through connected technologies.

One of the directive's key aspects applicable to connected devices is the safety of control systems and their ability to ensure safe and reliable operation. Manufacturers must ensure that control systems are designed to withstand potential cybersecurity threats and cannot be compromised by external attacks. While the Machinery Directive does not explicitly address cybersecurity, it does require that control systems pose no safety risks during operation and that manufacturers consider these threats as part of their risk assessment.

Another key aspect of the directive for connected devices is the obligation to conduct risk assessments. The directive requires manufacturers to perform a comprehensive risk assessment of the machine's use, including risks arising from the integration of connected technologies. This assessment must cover all phases of the product lifecycle, from installation and use to maintenance and disposal. For connected devices, this means evaluating risks related to remote access, the possibility of remote control, and interactions with other devices through a shared network. Manufacturers must identify and mitigate these risks by implementing measures such as isolating critical networks, real-time communication monitoring, and adopting security protocols for managing transmitted and received data.

Additionally, the technical documentation required by the directive must be adapted to include detailed information on the security of connections and interfaces with other systems. The regulation requires manufacturers to provide documentation detailing how the machine is designed to operate safely. For connected devices, this documentation must include information on adopted cybersecurity measures, communication protocols used, network interfaces, and software update procedures to ensure the device remains secure even after being placed on the market. While the directive does not directly address software updates, ensuring machines can be updated to address emerging security vulnerabilities is critical for connected devices.

The Machinery Directive also requires machines to be

equipped with emergency stop devices, which can be activated manually or automatically in the event of a malfunction. For connected devices, it is possible that machine control occurs remotely. Manufacturers must ensure that it is also possible to safely stop the machine in such cases. This may require implementing remote control systems that allow operators to intervene immediately in emergencies, even if they are not physically near the machine. Such systems must be designed to resist interruptions or external interference, ensuring that the emergency stop functions as intended.

Finally, data protection is a significant consideration. Although the directive does not directly address this issue, connected devices must still comply with European data protection regulations. Connected devices can collect and transmit data about users and their interactions with machines, making it essential to ensure such data is adequately protected. Manufacturers must ensure that data collected by connected devices is encrypted and processed in compliance with privacy regulations, especially if the devices collect personal data about operators or end users.

What are the CE marking requirements for new technologies?

CE marking requirements for new technologies fall within the broader framework of European Union regulations aimed at ensuring that products placed on the EU market meet specific standards of safety, health, and environmental protection. CE marking indicates that a product complies with applicable EU directives and regulations. It is mandatory for a wide range of products, including many new technologies such as connected devices, automated machinery, and products integrating artificial intelligence. While the requirements vary depending on the type of product and the applicable regulations, the general principles remain consistent.

One fundamental requirement for obtaining CE marking is

that the manufacturer or importer conducts a conformity assessment. This process ensures that the product meets all essential requirements set out in the applicable directives and regulations. For new technologies like IoT devices or AI-based systems, conformity requirements may include electrical safety, electromagnetic compatibility, functional safety, and protection against potential risks for end users. The manufacturer must issue an EU Declaration of Conformity certifying that the product complies with all applicable requirements and is ready for market entry.

A critical aspect of CE marking for new technologies involves functional safety. Many innovative technologies, such as automated machinery, robotic applications, or IoT devices, must ensure that their control and operating systems are safe and pose no risks to the health and safety of users. For instance, industrial robots must comply with the safety standards outlined in the Machinery Directive, which includes specific requirements for control systems such as emergency stops and protection against mechanical and electrical hazards. For new technologies, this may also include safeguards against software failures, update management, and mitigation of risks from unforeseen malfunctions.

Electromagnetic compatibility (EMC) is another key requirement for many technological products. This is especially relevant for electronic and connected devices, which must function properly in environments with other electronic devices without causing electromagnetic interference that could compromise their operation or that of nearby devices. The EMC Directive (2014/30/EU) requires that products neither generate unwanted electromagnetic interference nor be vulnerable to interference from other sources. For emerging technologies such as smart home devices, connected medical equipment, or IoT sensor networks, ensuring EMC compliance is essential to avoid malfunctions.

Another important requirement involves environmental protection and lifecycle management. Innovative products, such as those related to renewable energy technologies or electric vehicles, must comply with environmental regulations, including those on energy efficiency, waste management, and the use of hazardous substances. For example, the Energy Labelling Regulation (EU) 2017/1369 requires that certain technological products display their energy efficiency, helping consumers make more informed and sustainable choices. Additionally, the RoHS Directive (2011/65/EU) limits the use of hazardous substances like lead and mercury in electronic and technological products, which is particularly relevant for innovative devices containing electronic components.

To affix the CE marking, the manufacturer must compile a technical documentation file that includes all necessary information to demonstrate the product's compliance with applicable requirements.

This documentation must include:

- A detailed description of the product and its operation.

- Technical drawings and schematics of electrical or electronic circuits, if applicable.

- Risk assessments and measures taken to eliminate or mitigate risks.

- Test results demonstrating compliance, which may include internal tests conducted by the manufacturer or, in some cases, tests performed by independent notified bodies.

- User and maintenance manuals containing all necessary instructions for the safe use of the product.

For new technologies, the involvement of a notified body in the conformity assessment process may be required for some products. This is often the case for high-risk products such as medical devices, elevators, or certain complex industrial machinery. A notified body is a third-party organization that conducts independent assessments to verify that the product meets safety requirements. For many new technologies, such as connected medical devices or advanced automation systems, the involvement of a notified body can be crucial to ensuring that all critical functions, including software safety, are adequately evaluated.

Once the conformity assessment is complete and the technical documentation is prepared, the manufacturer can affix the CE marking to the product. The marking must be visible, legible, and indelible. It should be placed on the product itself and, where possible, on the packaging or accompanying documents. The CE marking signifies that the product can be legally sold within the European single market.

How can the security risks of products incorporating artificial intelligence be managed?

Managing the security risks associated with products incorporating artificial intelligence (AI) has become a central priority for businesses and regulators, especially given the increasing adoption of these technologies in critical sectors such as healthcare, industrial production, and transportation. AI's ability to analyze real-time data, make autonomous decisions, and improve operational efficiency introduces a new dimension of complexity and risk, including physical safety for users, data security, and privacy protection.

The first fundamental step in managing security risks in AI-integrated products is to conduct a comprehensive risk assessment throughout the product's lifecycle. This assessment must consider both traditional risks (such as mechanical failures or operational errors) and new risks introduced by AI, such as system behavior unpredictability and potential vulnerabilities to cyberattacks. An effective risk assessment should include identifying threats, estimating their likelihood, analyzing potential consequences, and planning mitigation measures. For example, if an AI product is used in an industrial context, it is necessary to consider the risk of the AI making incorrect decisions during critical operations, which could impact worker safety or machine integrity.

A key component in managing risks in AI products is ensuring transparency and traceability of the algorithms used. AI technologies, particularly machine learning systems, can act autonomously and learn from the data they are trained on. This can lead to behavior that is not always predictable, especially if the AI is exposed to new data or scenarios not considered during training. To mitigate this risk, AI systems should be designed with transparency, allowing operators to trace decision-making pathways. Adopting the principle of "explainability" ensures that AI decisions are understandable, monitorable, and adjustable if necessary. For instance, in an autonomous driving system, it is crucial to trace and explain why the AI made a particular maneuver in a specific situation, especially during the training phase.

Human oversight mechanisms are another important strategy for managing security risks. Even though AI-based products are designed to be autonomous, there must always be the possibility of human intervention in critical situations. This can be achieved through control systems that allow human operators to monitor the AI in real-time and intervene to modify its actions if unexpected or dangerous behavior occurs. For high-risk AI systems, such as those used in industrial robotics or healthcare, regulators may require the presence of a "human-in-the-loop" or a human supervisor who can halt or correct the AI's operations when necessary.

Cybersecurity is another critical aspect of managing risks in AI products. These products, often connected to external networks and systems, are vulnerable to various cybersecurity threats, such as targeted attacks that manipulate algorithms or alter the data underlying AI decision-making. A cyberattack on an AI system could have disastrous consequences, especially in critical applications such as energy infrastructure, public transportation, or medical devices. To mitigate this risk, advanced cybersecurity measures must be adopted, including data encryption, multi factor authentication, network segmentation, and continuous monitoring for suspicious activity. AI systems must also be designed to withstand manipulation attempts or "data poisoning," where attackers introduce malicious data into the training set to compromise the algorithm's behavior.

Special attention must be paid to the security of the data used by AI. AI-based products often rely on large datasets to train and improve their algorithms. This can include personal, sensitive, or confidential data, as is the case with AI systems used in healthcare or finance. It is essential to handle this data in compliance with privacy regulations, such as the GDPR. Manufacturers must ensure that data used by AI is adequately protected through measures like anonymization, minimization of data collection, and secure storage practices.

Validation and continuous testing of AI systems are also crucial strategies for managing security risks. Before launching an AI-based product on the market, rigorous testing and statistical performance checks are essential to ensure it functions as intended and does not exhibit undesirable or dangerous behaviors. This process includes robustness testing to evaluate how AI responds to anomalous data or unforeseen events and verifying its ability to maintain safe performance over time. Since AI can evolve and improve through learning, implementing post-market monitoring systems is necessary to detect behavioral changes and address issues promptly.

Collaboration with regulatory authorities and adherence to internationally recognized safety standards are, of course, essential for managing the risks of AI products. The European Union, through initiatives like the Artificial Intelligence Act, is working to create a regulatory framework that ensures the safety and reliability of AI-based products. Operators must ensure their products comply with these regulations and meet established safety standards.

What are the safety standards for chains and ropes used in lifting systems?

Chains and ropes used in lifting systems are critical components for ensuring the safety and efficiency of operations involving heavy load lifting. In recent years, evolving European and international regulations have introduced new specific standards governing the safety and usage of these equipment. These standards aim to ensure that chains and ropes used in lifting systems are designed, manufactured, and maintained according to strict criteria to prevent accidents and protect operators.

One of the primary regulatory frameworks governing the safety of chains and ropes is the Machinery Directive. While this directive covers a broad spectrum of machinery, it includes specific provisions for lifting systems such as cranes, hoists, and other load-handling devices. The directive mandates that components used in lifting systems, including chains and ropes, must be designed to withstand specific loads and ensure there is no risk of failure or malfunction under normal use.

Chains and ropes must comply with harmonized European standards such as EN 818 and EN 12385, which specify technical requirements for the design, manufacture, testing, and maintenance of chains and ropes used in lifting applications.

These standards address various aspects, including:

Materials and manufacturing
The standards specify the materials that can be used for manufacturing chains and ropes, such as high-strength steel, and the mechanical properties required to withstand specified loads. Mechanical tests, such as tensile strength tests, must be conducted to verify that chains and ropes can handle maximum

rated loads without deformation or failure.

Safety factor
A critical element of the standards is adherence to an appropriate safety factor, representing the ratio between the working load limit (WLL) and the minimum breaking load (MBL). For example, chains and ropes used in lifting systems must have a high enough safety factor to ensure they can endure stress conditions without failure, even during temporary overloads.

Inspections and maintenance
The standards emphasize the importance of regular inspections and preventive maintenance. Equipment must be routinely inspected for signs of wear, corrosion, or damage that could compromise safety. EN 818, for instance, requires that lifting chains undergo visual inspections and non-destructive testing to ensure there are no structural defects.

Marking and traceability
Another essential requirement is the mandatory marking of chains and ropes. Each chain or rope used in a lifting system must be clearly marked with relevant information such as the WLL, manufacturer details, material type, and identification number. Marking ensures the traceability of components, allowing operators to verify that the equipment is suitable for the intended load.

Initial testing and certification
Chains and ropes must undergo initial testing and certification before being used in lifting systems. Tests may include tensile strength testing, fatigue testing, and break tests to ensure the product can withstand real operational conditions without failure. Additionally, some lifting systems require periodic testing to ensure lifting capacity remains consistent over time.

Resistance to environmental conditions
Chains and ropes used in challenging environments, such as those exposed to extreme weather, corrosive agents, or high temperatures, must be designed to withstand such stresses. The standards specify requirements to ensure equipment used in these conditions is made from materials resistant to corrosion and thermal variations, guaranteeing operational safety and longevity.

How can safety standards be ensured for products imported from third countries?

Ensuring safety standards for products imported from third countries is a priority for the European Union, committed to protecting consumers and operators within the single market. Products from non-EU countries must meet the same safety, quality, and compliance requirements as those manufactured in the EU. Achieving this objective relies on a regulatory framework combining border controls, economic operator responsibilities, international cooperation, and market surveillance.

The Market Surveillance Regulation (EU) 2019/1020, effective from 2021, enhances control over products entering the EU market by imposing stricter obligations on importers and distributors. Importers are responsible for ensuring that products from third countries comply with EU regulations before they are placed on the market. This includes verifying the presence of the CE marking, which certifies product conformity with applicable EU directives and regulations, such as the Machinery Directive, REACH Regulation for chemicals, RoHS Directive for hazardous substances in electronics, and others.

Importers must ensure that imported products are accompanied by an EU Declaration of Conformity and appropriate technical documentation, which must be available upon request by market surveillance authorities. The technical documentation must include all necessary information to demonstrate compliance with essential safety requirements, such as laboratory test reports, risk assessment results, technical drawings, and conformity certificates issued by notified bodies, if applicable. Importers are also required to retain this documentation for at least 10 years after the product is placed on the market, ensuring that authorities can verify compliance over time.

Ensuring the safety of imported products requires traceability throughout the supply chain. According to EU regulations, each imported product must be clearly identifiable through a serial number or specific code. It must also include the manufacturer's name and address, as well as information about the importer or distributor responsible for placing it on the EU market. This traceability allows for the swift identification of non-compliant or hazardous products and enables corrective actions, such as market recalls or sales suspensions, in case of safety issues.

Collaboration among market surveillance authorities in EU member states is crucial for ensuring the safety of imported products. ICSMS (Information and Communication System on Market Surveillance), established under Regulation (EU) 2019/1020, facilitates the real-time exchange of information on non-compliant or hazardous products. This system enables national authorities to monitor products entering the EU and take swift action when non-compliant items are detected. Additionally, EU customs authorities play a central role in inspecting imported products and blocking the entry of non-compliant or potentially hazardous goods.

For certain high-risk products, such as medical devices, complex industrial machinery, or chemicals, notified bodies must evaluate compliance before the products are placed on the EU market. These independent organizations conduct tests and conformity assessments to verify that products meet safety requirements under EU directives. Importers must ensure that products from third countries undergo these assessments where required and possess all necessary certificates.

Educating economic operators throughout the supply chain

is essential for ensuring the safety of imported products. Importers, distributors, and other stakeholders must be adequately informed about the safety and compliance requirements they need to meet. Obligations include training on EU regulations, proper handling of technical documentation, and understanding the risks associated with non-compliant products. Market surveillance authorities play a key role in providing guidelines and information to economic operators, ensuring they understand their responsibilities and take preventive measures to avoid importing unsafe products.

International cooperation with exporting countries is vital to ensure that imported products comply with EU safety standards. The EU collaborates with third countries through trade agreements and technical cooperation programs that promote harmonization of safety standards and conformity assessment procedures. These agreements may include mutual recognition of conformity certificates, facilitating market access for goods while upholding EU safety standards.

7. AI ACT AND NEW EUROPEAN FRAMEWORK

What principles are established by Regulation (EU) 2024/1689 to promote human-centric, safe, and rights-respecting artificial intelligence?

Regulation (EU) 2024/1689, known as the AI Act, introduces guiding principles to ensure the development of human-centric, safe, and rights-respecting artificial intelligence (AI) that aligns with the fundamental values of the European Union. The human-centered approach places individuals at the core: AI must be designed and used as a tool that not only supports but also respects and promotes human well-being, autonomy, and dignity. To this end, the regulation mandates that AI systems must always operate transparently, traceably, and securely.

These principles are closely tied to the values enshrined in the EU Charter of Fundamental Rights, which include the protection of human dignity, the right to private and family life, the protection of personal data, non-discrimination, and respect for the rights of children. The AI Act emphasizes that any AI system used within European territory must operate in a way that upholds these rights. To achieve this, the regulation introduces a risk-based classification of AI systems, with stricter obligations for high-risk systems, including rigorous requirements for transparency, technical robustness, and reliability.

Key guiding principles also include a prohibition on manipulative and discriminatory practices and a requirement for human oversight to prevent misuse or uncontrolled autonomy of AI systems. To this end, the regulation explicitly refers to the ethical guidelines for trustworthy AI developed by the EU High-Level Expert Group on Artificial Intelligence (AI HLEG), incorporating principles such as transparency,

non-discrimination and fairness, accountability, and technical robustness.
Finally, the AI Act integrates its guiding principles with specific regulatory obligations, such as those concerning AI systems that pose privacy risks, in alignment with the General Data Protection Regulation (GDPR). This complementary approach creates a coherent European regulatory ecosystem where technological innovation can flourish without compromising the rights and security of European citizens.

How does the Regulation harmonize national legislation across member states to prevent market fragmentation?

The AI Act aims to establish a harmonized regulatory framework to prevent fragmentation in AI regulations across EU Member States. A key objective of the regulation is to ensure uniform rules for AI throughout the European Union, avoiding divergent national laws that could undermine the internal market and hinder the free flow of AI-based products and services.

To achieve this, the regulation implements a series of standardized measures requiring Member States to adopt a unified and coordinated approach. Central to this is the establishment of harmonized requirements for the deployment, commercialization, and use of AI systems. These requirements include criteria for transparency, robustness, and safety, with a particular focus on high-risk systems. This approach fosters a regulatory environment where businesses can operate within a single market under consistent rules, avoiding the need to comply with varying national regulations.

The regulation also safeguards the free movement of AI systems, making it unlawful for Member States to impose restrictions on the distribution or use of AI systems that comply with the AI Act. Exceptions to this freedom are permitted only when explicitly provided for in the regulation and justified by legitimate public interest objectives.

To facilitate harmonization, the regulation establishes a European AI Board tasked with coordinating and overseeing the uniform application of rules across Member States. This body works closely with national market surveillance authorities to ensure consistent interpretation and enforcement of the regulation throughout the EU.

The harmonized approach of the AI Act fits into a broader framework of European digital policies, such as the GDPR, the Digital Services Act (DSA), and the Digital Markets Act (DMA). These legislative instruments are designed to operate in synergy, promoting legal certainty and creating a stable and uniform market environment for companies developing and using digital technologies in the EU.

What AI practices are deemed unacceptable and prohibited by the Regulation?

Regulation (EU) 2024/1689 identifies certain AI practices as unacceptable and explicitly prohibits their use to protect EU citizens from serious risks to their rights and fundamental values. These practices are considered contrary to the ethical principles underpinning the regulation, in line with the guidelines for trustworthy AI established in 2019 by the AI HLEG.

The prohibited practices include:
Psychological and Behavioral Manipulation
AI systems designed to exploit cognitive or social vulnerabilities to influence behavior unconsciously are banned. For example, using subliminal stimuli to drive individuals toward decisions they would not otherwise make compromises their autonomy and is prohibited.

Exploit of specific vulnerabilities

The regulation forbids the use of AI systems that exploit vulnerabilities related to age, disability, or economic or social conditions if such exploitation could cause significant harm to individuals or vulnerable groups. This prohibition extends to cases where vulnerable individuals (such as children or those in economic distress) are subjected to persuasive or exploitative AI techniques that lead to harmful behaviors.

Social scoring
The use of AI systems to classify individuals based on social scoring, attributed according to behavior or personal characteristics, is prohibited. These systems, which evaluate individuals based on a range of parameters unrelated to the context of use, can lead to discrimination and unfair treatment in unrelated domains.

Remote real-time biometric identification in public spaces
The use of AI systems for remote real-time biometric identification in public spaces is banned, with narrowly defined exceptions, such as immediate threats to public security. This prohibition reflects the invasive potential of such systems, which can undermine citizens' privacy and limit their freedom of movement and assembly, creating a sense of constant surveillance.

These prohibited practices align with the seven ethical principles outlined by the AI HLEG for trustworthy AI:

- Human agency and oversight
- Technical robustness and safety
- Privacy and data governance
- Transparency
- Diversity and non-discrimination
- Societal and environmental well-being
- Accountability

The bans on manipulative practices and exploitation of vulnerabilities, for instance, uphold the principles of autonomy and human dignity, while the prohibitions on social scoring and remote biometric identification protect non-discrimination and privacy. In this way, the AI Act not only establishes stringent guidelines for the responsible use of AI but also reaffirms the EU's commitment to building AI systems that respect and protect fundamental rights, aligning with the ethical and social expectations of European citizens.

How do the rules of the new Regulation integrate with the GDPR and the processing of personal data in AI systems?

Regulation (EU) 2024/1689 on Artificial Intelligence and the GDPR are closely interlinked, particularly concerning the use and processing of personal data in AI systems. Both aim to safeguard the fundamental rights of individuals but take complementary approaches.

The AI Act establishes specific rules for AI systems that process personal data, requiring their use to align with the GDPR's principles of lawfulness, fairness, transparency, and data minimization. The GDPR mandates that personal data should only be processed for clear and legitimate purposes and that excessive data collection must be avoided. The AI Act strengthens these principles by imposing stringent requirements on AI systems for transparency and traceability, ensuring that individuals are aware of when and how their data is being used.

One key area of integration between the two regulations is automated decision-making and profiling. The GDPR protects individuals from being subject to decisions solely based on automated processing that produce legal or similarly significant effects (Article 22 GDPR). The AI Act further requires that high-risk AI systems provide adequate human oversight, ensuring that decisions are not fully delegated to machines and allowing intervention in cases of errors or biases. This reduces the risk of individuals being subjected to unfair or discriminatory decisions based solely on AI outputs.

Another overlap concerns the protection of biometric data and facial recognition. The AI Act severely restricts or bans the use of AI systems for remote biometric surveillance in real-time, introducing provisions that bolster the protections already established by the GDPR. The use of biometric data, such as facial recognition, is deemed highly invasive to individuals' privacy and is therefore strictly regulated under both frameworks.

The AI Act also sets transparency and explainability requirements that align with the GDPR's right to information (Articles 13 and 14), obliging users to be informed about how AI systems process their data, including the risks and limitations of these systems. Operators must document the functioning of high-risk AI systems and ensure that this information is accessible and understandable, even to non-experts. These obligations are crucial for enabling individuals to exercise their rights of access, rectification, or deletion of personal data, as provided by the GDPR.

Finally, the GDPR assigns data protection authorities the responsibility of overseeing compliance with personal data regulations. The AI Act reinforces this mechanism by involving national data protection authorities in monitoring AI systems that process personal data, ensuring that GDPR principles are upheld in the deployment and management of AI systems.

Together, the AI Act and the GDPR create a comprehensive and coherent regulatory framework that promotes technological innovation while preserving the fundamental rights of citizens.

What is the regulator's approach to high-risk AI systems?

Regulation (EU) 2024/1689 adopts a risk-based approach to

regulate AI systems, classifying them based on their potential impact on fundamental rights, safety, and citizen well-being. For high-risk AI systems, the regulation imposes stringent requirements to ensure transparency, security, reliability, and appropriate human oversight. This approach allows for proportional regulation of different AI types, with stricter rules for applications posing significant risks.

Criteria for the classification and compliance of high-risk AI systems
A system is classified as "high-risk" if it has a significant impact on sensitive areas such as healthcare, education, employment, justice administration, and law enforcement. Examples include AI systems used for medical diagnosis, personnel selection, student evaluation, or real-time remote biometric surveillance. The European Commission issues updated guidelines to identify and classify high-risk AI systems, ensuring the regulation remains adaptable to technological advancements.

Specific obligations for high-risk AI systems
Providers of high-risk AI systems must comply with several requirements to place their systems on the EU market, including:

- *Data management and risk minimization*
Data used for training and operating high-risk AI systems must be high-quality, representative, and bias-free to minimize discrimination risks and ensure fairness.

- *Transparency and user information*
Providers must inform end-users and affected individuals about the AI's use, explicitly detailing its functioning, limitations, and potential risks. This includes maintaining technical documentation accessible for regulatory inspections.

- *Human oversight and control*
High-risk AI systems must allow adequate human supervision

to prevent fully automated decisions without intervention. Organizations must ensure that operators have the necessary control to prevent errors or misuse and intervene in case of malfunctions.

- Robustness and security
Systems must be designed to withstand attacks and errors, ensuring accuracy and security even in critical situations. Providers must conduct rigorous testing to verify reliability and robustness, preventing malfunctions that could cause significant harm.

- Monitoring and reporting
Operators of high-risk AI systems are required to continuously monitor system performance and report any anomalies or malfunctions to competent authorities. Additionally, in case of serious incidents or security breaches, they must implement reporting and risk mitigation procedures.

- Conformity assessment and registration
High-risk AI systems must undergo a conformity assessment before entering the market. This process may include internal checks or third-party oversight. Successfully assessed systems are registered in a centralized database managed by the European Commission, accessible to national data protection authorities and other relevant supervisory bodies.

Relevance of requirements for fundamental rights and ethical principles
The requirements for high-risk AI systems are designed to safeguard fundamental rights, ensuring that technological applications do not compromise individuals' privacy, safety, or dignity. The regulation's approach is inspired by the EU's ethical principles for trustworthy AI, including transparency, non-discrimination, and human dignity. Human oversight and transparency are central to avoiding citizen exposure to

uncontrolled automated decisions, minimizing risks of bias or unfair treatment.

How does the regulation govern biometric AI systems?

Regulation (EU) 2024/1689 introduces specific rules for artificial intelligence (AI) systems that use biometric data, such as facial recognition, emotion detection, and biometric categorization. Given their potential intrusiveness and impact on fundamental rights, particularly privacy, these systems are classified as high-risk and are subject to stringent restrictions and requirements to ensure their use is safe and respects individual freedoms.

Regulation of biometric AI systems
Biometric AI systems can be used to identify, monitor, or categorize individuals based on physical or behavioral characteristics such as facial features, voice, or fingerprints. However, the regulation imposes strict limits to prevent these tools from violating privacy or enabling mass surveillance, restricting their use to specific contexts and under defined conditions:

- Prohibition of remote biometric surveillance in real-time in public spaces
The regulation prohibits the use of real-time remote biometric recognition systems in publicly accessible spaces for surveillance or identification purposes, except under extraordinary circumstances. These exceptions are limited to scenarios such as imminent threats to public safety, including terrorist attacks or locating missing persons. Even in such cases, strict safeguards must be in place, such as prior authorization from a judicial authority.

- Emotion recognition and biometric categorization

The AI Act severely limits the use of systems designed to identify emotions or categorize individuals based on biometric data. These systems cannot classify individuals based on personal attributes such as ethnicity, sexual orientation, or religious beliefs, aligning with the principles of non-discrimination and dignity outlined in the EU Charter of Fundamental Rights. Such tools may only be used in specific contexts with justified purposes, ensuring privacy and individual freedoms are never compromised.

- *Transparency and information*
Users and individuals must be informed when AI systems process their biometric data. Providers of such systems are required to supply clear and accessible documentation explaining how the system works, its intended purpose, associated risks, and the measures implemented to minimize negative impacts on privacy and rights.

Integration with the GDPR and other European laws
Regulation (EU) 2024/1689 complements the GDPR and Directive (EU) 2016/680, which governs the processing of personal data for law enforcement and security purposes. Both frameworks establish strict rules for processing biometric data, categorizing it as sensitive data requiring specific protection measures.

The GDPR mandates that biometric data may only be processed with clear consent from the individual or for significant public interest. The AI Act strengthens these provisions by imposing additional obligations on providers of biometric AI systems. It also requires oversight and auditing by national data protection authorities to ensure compliance with privacy regulations. This integration ensures that biometric data processing respects individuals' rights and allows authorities to intervene if AI systems breach established rules.

Security measures and technical requirements

To prevent discrimination or privacy violations, the regulation requires biometric AI systems to be designed with high standards of security and reliability. Providers must ensure that biometric data is accurate, relevant, and up-to-date to minimize errors and false positives. Additionally, the system must undergo rigorous and periodic technical evaluations to verify compliance with regulations and prevent adverse impacts.

Protection of fundamental rights and ethical principles
Through these provisions, the AI Act aims to protect citizens' fundamental rights, including privacy, data protection, and non-discrimination. The limits imposed on biometric AI systems reflect the EU's ethical approach to artificial intelligence, which must be safe, transparent, and respectful of human dignity.

How is the use of real-time biometric identification systems in public spaces for security and law enforcement regulated?

Regulation (EU) 2024/1689 imposes strict restrictions on using real-time biometric identification systems in public spaces for security and law enforcement, acknowledging the invasive potential of such technologies on privacy and fundamental rights. Real-time biometric identification is particularly sensitive as it can lead to mass surveillance, infringing on individuals' privacy, freedom of movement, and freedom of assembly.

General Ban and Limited Exceptions
The regulation establishes a general prohibition on using remote real-time biometric identification systems in public spaces for law enforcement purposes. However, narrowly defined exceptions allow their use under specific and strictly regulated conditions:

- Preventing imminent threats to life or physical safety
For example, during immediate risks of terrorist attacks or other public safety emergencies, biometric identification technologies may be authorized to facilitate rapid identification and intervention by authorities.

- Locating missing persons, including minors or vulnerable individuals
In emergencies, such as finding missing persons, authorities may use these technologies to identify and locate individuals in danger.

- Identifying perpetrators or suspects of serious crimes
Biometric identification may be authorized to track suspects of severe crimes punishable by at least four years of imprisonment, as defined by national laws and the offenses listed in the regulation.

Authorization conditions and procedural safeguards
To use these systems, prior authorization from a judicial or independent administrative authority is mandatory, and such authorization must be binding. Each case must have a specific purpose and clearly defined usage limits. In extraordinary emergencies where prior authorization is not possible, the regulation allows temporary use of AI systems, provided authorization is sought as soon as possible and within 24 hours. The use of these systems must be proportionate and geographically and temporally limited: the duration and area of surveillance must be strictly confined to what is necessary to address the specific threat. Additionally, the biometric data collected must be processed and stored following personal data protection regulations, including the GDPR and other privacy and security provisions.

Impact assessment on fundamental rights

Before authorizing real-time biometric identification in public spaces, competent authorities must conduct a fundamental rights impact assessment to evaluate the potential consequences of using the system on privacy, freedom of movement, and other rights. This assessment is crucial to ensure that the technology's use does not lead to discrimination or biases against specific groups.

Transparency and oversight
The regulation mandates that every use of real-time remote biometric identification be recorded in a centralized database and supervised by national data protection authorities and market surveillance authorities. These authorities must submit annual reports to the European Commission on the use of such technologies, ensuring transparency and accountability in implementing these extraordinary measures.

Protection of fundamental rights
These rules reflect the EU's strong commitment to protecting fundamental rights and ensuring that surveillance technologies are used only in exceptional cases with appropriate safeguards. The AI Act seeks to balance public safety and citizens' privacy by preventing mass surveillance and promoting a proportionate and responsible use of technology.

What incentives or support measures for responsible AI innovation are available to SMEs and start-ups?

The AI Act not only establishes compliance rules for the use of artificial intelligence but also includes support measures and incentives aimed at promoting responsible innovation in Europe. In particular, the regulation recognizes the importance of small and medium-sized enterprises (SMEs) and start-ups, which are a crucial part of the European tech landscape and play a key role in developing innovative AI solutions. To this end, the AI Act introduces initiatives to foster the growth of these businesses while ensuring adherence to safety and transparency standards.

Support measures for SMEs and start-ups

- Financial support and innovation incentives
The AI Act provides for the establishment of specific funding programs to support the research, development, and testing of AI solutions by SMEs and start-ups. Through these funds, the European Union aims to help small businesses overcome financial barriers associated with implementing AI systems that meet the regulation's technical requirements. These funding programs, often co-financed by Member States, aim to cover part of the compliance costs, allowing companies to focus on innovation without bearing the entire financial burden.

- Regulatory sandboxes
The AI Act introduces regulatory sandboxes—protected environments where businesses, especially SMEs and start-ups, can test their AI systems under the supervision of competent authorities. Within these sandboxes, companies can develop and experiment with new technologies without being immediately subject to all applicable regulatory requirements. Regulatory sandboxes provide an innovation-friendly setting to verify compliance with regulations flexibly and with support from oversight authorities.

- Technical assistance and compliance guidelines
The AI Act mandates that European and national authorities provide technical assistance and specific guidelines to facilitate understanding and application of the regulations. These resources, particularly targeted at SMEs, are essential to clarify compliance requirements and reduce regulatory complexity, which can be challenging for smaller businesses with limited resources. Technical assistance may include operational manuals, training, and consultations to help SMEs develop AI

products compliant from the initial stages of the project.

- Reduced compliance burdens
To prevent the regulation's requirements from being overly burdensome for SMEs, the AI Act includes specific measures for regulatory simplification, adapting some compliance obligations to the size and capacity of businesses. For instance, SMEs may benefit from simplified conformity assessment processes or extended adjustment periods. This flexibility is designed to support small businesses without compromising the safety and reliability standards required by the regulation.

Innovation ecosystem and European cooperation
The regulation also promotes collaboration among businesses, universities, and research centers, encouraging the sharing of resources and knowledge to accelerate AI innovation. Public-private partnerships and joint research programs are encouraged to help SMEs develop cutting-edge technologies while adopting ethical and transparent standards.
Additionally, the AI Act involves the European Artificial Intelligence Board, tasked with monitoring and coordinating support initiatives for innovation and promoting best practices among Member States. Through European-level cooperation, the regulation aims to create an inclusive and competitive innovation ecosystem, enabling the EU to become a global leader in AI.

Promotion of ethical and sustainable AI
Finally, the AI Act encourages the development of ethical and sustainable AI, requiring businesses to integrate ethical principles and transparency into their systems from the design phase. This approach is reflected in the funding criteria and support program access requirements, rewarding companies committed to respecting values such as human rights protection, non-discrimination, and environmental responsibility. SMEs and start-ups adhering to these principles

can access specific incentives and gain a competitive edge in the European market.

How does the regulation relate to the Digital Services Act and Digital Markets Act?

Regulation (EU) 2024/1689 integrates with other key EU regulations, such as the Digital Services Act (DSA) and the Digital Markets Act (DMA), to build a cohesive and comprehensive regulatory framework governing the digital transformation in Europe. Each regulation addresses specific aspects of the digital world, but together they promote innovation, ensure safety, and protect European citizens' rights within the digital ecosystem.

Digital Services Act (DSA) and AI Act
The DSA focuses on regulating digital services, particularly online platforms, aiming to enhance user safety and limit the spread of illegal content. It imposes transparency, accountability, and content moderation obligations on digital platforms, requiring large platforms to prevent service misuse and protect users. This regulation is particularly relevant for platforms integrating AI to manage content, recommend information, or filter harmful materials.
The AI Act complements the DSA by regulating AI systems used for content moderation and user protection online. For example, if a platform uses AI algorithms to filter illegal content or classify information, such systems must comply with the AI Act's provisions, particularly if classified as high-risk systems. The DSA and AI Act thus work hand-in-hand: the DSA governs the general framework of digital services, while the AI Act specifically addresses requirements for the AI used in these contexts, ensuring it is transparent, safe, and rights-compliant.
Both regulations demand transparency in the use of algorithms and AI to ensure users are informed about automated decisions affecting them and can understand how these mechanisms

operate. This synergy provides users with greater protections while offering businesses a clear and predictable regulatory framework.

Digital Markets Act (DMA) and AI Act
The DMA aims to regulate digital "gatekeepers," or large platforms that, due to their size and influence, control access to significant portions of the digital market. The DMA seeks to prevent anti-competitive practices, ensuring a level playing field and protecting consumer rights. Gatekeepers, such as major search engines and social media platforms, often influence how digital goods and services are accessed, including those involving AI systems integrated into their services.

The AI Act and DMA are complementary because, while the DMA prevents dominant platforms from abusing their market power, the AI Act ensures the AI used by these platforms is safe, ethical, and non-discriminatory. For instance, if a gatekeeper platform uses AI systems to rank providers or favor its services, such algorithms must comply with the AI Act's principles, such as fairness, transparency, and the prevention of discriminatory or biased behavior. This joint approach enhances transparency and competitiveness in the market, ensuring AI is not used in ways that harm consumers or industry players.

Building a cohesive regulatory framework
Together, the AI Act, DSA, and DMA create a European regulatory ecosystem that promotes an innovative, open, and secure digital market where both large platforms and small businesses must adhere to high standards of accountability and transparency.

This combination of regulations aims to:

- Protecting users' rights
The DSA and AI Act work to ensure users are informed and protected, especially when their online interactions are mediated by AI algorithms. Transparency about the use of AI

on digital platforms and the ability to understand and challenge automated decisions are fundamental principles for effective user protection.

- Promoting fair competition and preventing market power abuse
Through the DMA, the EU regulates gatekeeper behavior, while the AI Act ensures the AI systems facilitating these interactions comply with ethical and safety standards. This joint framework reduces the risk of consumers and small competitors being disadvantaged by AI and discriminatory algorithms used by dominant platforms.

- Encouraging responsible innovation
The three regulations foster a responsible and secure innovation environment. The AI Act provides businesses, particularly SMEs and start-ups, with the support needed to develop new AI solutions that comply with European rules, creating a market that supports innovation without compromising individual rights and competition.

What are the consequences and obligations for ai providers based outside the EU whose systems have effects within the Union?

Regulation (EU) 2024/1689 on artificial intelligence establishes specific obligations for AI providers based outside the European Union whose systems produce effects within the EU. This extraterritorial scope reflects the Union's commitment to protecting the rights of European citizens and creating a transparent and secure technological market, regardless of the geographical origin of AI providers. External providers must comply with the AI Act's requirements if their systems are intended for use within the Union, even if developed or operated outside its borders.

Obligations for non-EU providers

Non-European AI providers are subject to several obligations when their AI systems are used within the EU. Key requirements include:

- Designation of a representative

AI providers operating from non-EU countries must designate a representative within the Union. The representative serves as the point of contact for supervisory authorities and European users and is responsible for ensuring compliance with the AI Act. The representative may be held liable for the provider's non-compliance, increasing accountability and facilitating enforcement of the rules within the EU.

- Compliance with high-risk system requirements

If an AI system provided by a non-EU operator is classified as high-risk, the provider must ensure that the system meets all regulatory requirements, including transparency, safety, and human oversight. For instance, external providers must technically document the system, perform conformity assessments, and demonstrate that their product meets the robustness and reliability standards required for high-risk systems.

- Transparency and user information

Non-EU providers must ensure transparency about their systems, informing users about the purposes and limitations of the AI being used. This transparency obligation ensures that European users understand the operation and potential risks of the AI, particularly in contexts where these technologies directly affect individual rights or decisions.

- Conformity assessment and registration

Non-EU providers of high-risk AI systems must undergo a conformity assessment to ensure that the system meets the safety and transparency standards established by the AI Act.

Once the assessment is passed, the system is registered in a centralized EU database accessible to European oversight authorities. This step is crucial for effective supervision of AI systems, even when the provider is not physically present within the Union.

- Incident and anomaly reporting obligation
In the event of malfunctions or significant incidents involving the AI system, non-EU providers must promptly notify the competent European authorities, enabling a rapid and appropriate response. This obligation aims to protect the safety and rights of European citizens, allowing authorities to monitor and intervene in case of critical issues.

Extraterritorial enforcement and international cooperation
The extraterritorial scope of the AI Act aims to prevent external AI providers from circumventing European regulations simply by operating from third countries. The regulation allows for the possibility of sanctioning non-compliant providers, even when they are based outside the EU. European supervisory authorities can collaborate with authorities in third countries to ensure that AI systems sold or used in Europe comply with EU norms. Additionally, the Union promotes international cooperation agreements to align AI regulatory standards, fostering a shared global regulatory context.

Market impact and protection of European citizens
These provisions are essential to ensuring that European citizens are protected from the potentially negative effects of AI, even when such systems originate from non-EU countries. Through uniform application of the rules, the AI Act preserves user trust and creates fair competition conditions for all businesses operating within the Union. The regulatory framework ensures that all AI systems sold and used in Europe meet high standards of safety and rights protection, regardless of their geographical origin.

CONCLUSIONS

This volume provides a comprehensive guide to European regulations on digital innovation, with a focus on the legal aspects of rapidly evolving fields such as artificial intelligence, data protection, and cybersecurity. It addresses a wide range of topics, including the rights and responsibilities of stakeholders in digital transformation, privacy safeguards, and an analysis of regulatory frameworks shaping markets and advanced technological activities.

The goal is to present an accessible yet detailed overview of the rules impacting digital technologies, offering critical insights into existing provisions, potential risks, and opportunities for various actors. In a landscape where technology progresses faster than regulation, the book underscores the pivotal role of law in safeguarding safety and individual rights while fostering innovation.

Among the subjects covered, the European regulation on artificial intelligence stands out as a landmark initiative by the European Union to establish a harmonized and secure framework for the development and use of AI. This pioneering regulation introduces unified rules to address ethical and practical challenges posed by AI, outlining criteria to classify and manage risks associated with AI systems across diverse sectors, including sensitive areas like healthcare, automation, and robotics.

However, the regulation on AI is not the central focus of this book, as its implementation is still in progress and its provisions are not yet fully enforceable. As of autumn 2024, most businesses and professionals in the AI sector are not subject to its requirements. For this reason, the discussion prioritizes other legal areas that are already fully operational and significant for stakeholders. A dedicated exploration of the AI regulation may follow in the near future, offering a more detailed analysis of its applications and implications across various fields.

REGULATIONS AND STANDARDS

European Regulations

Directive 2006/42/EC of the European Parliament and of the Council of 17 May 2006 on machinery, amending Directive 95/16/EC (Machinery Directive).

Directive 2011/65/EU of the European Parliament and of the Council of 8 June 2011 on the restriction of the use of certain hazardous substances in electrical and electronic equipment (RoHS Directive).

General Data Protection Regulation (GDPR): Regulation (EU) 2016/679 of the European Parliament and of the Council of 27 April 2016 on the protection of natural persons with regard to the processing of personal data and on the free movement of such data.

Regulation (EU) 2017/745 of the European Parliament and of the Council of 5 April 2017 on medical devices, repealing Council Directives 93/42/EEC and 90/385/EEC.

Regulation (EU) 2017/1369 of the European Parliament and of the Council of 4 July 2017 establishing a framework for energy labeling and repealing Directive 2010/30/EU.

Regulation (EU) 2019/881 of the European Parliament and of the Council of 17 April 2019 on the European Union Agency for Cybersecurity (ENISA) and on information and communications technology cybersecurity certification.

Regulation (EU) 2019/1020 of the European Parliament and of the Council of 20 June 2019 on market surveillance and product compliance, amending Directive 2004/42/EC, Regulation (EC)

No 765/2008, and Regulation (EU) No 305/2011.

Directive (EU) 2019/1937 of the European Parliament and of the Council of 23 October 2019 on the protection of persons who report breaches of Union law (Whistleblowing Directive).

Regulation (EU) 2023/1230 of the European Parliament and of the Council of 14 June 2023 on machinery, repealing Directive 2006/42/EC.

Regulation (EU) 2024/1689 of the European Parliament and of the Council of 13 June 2024 establishing harmonized rules on artificial intelligence, amending Regulations (EC) No 300/2008, (EU) No 167/2013, (EU) No 168/2013, (EU) 2018/858, (EU) 2018/1139, and (EU) 2019/2144, and Directives 2014/90/EU, (EU) 2016/797, and (EU) 2020/1828 (Artificial Intelligence Regulation).

Regulation (EU) 2022/2065 of the European Parliament and of the Council of 19 October 2022 on a single market for digital services, amending Directive 2000/31/EC (Digital Services Regulation).

Regulation (EU) 2022/1925 of the European Parliament and of the Council of 14 September 2022 on contestable and fair markets in the digital sector, amending Directives (EU) 2019/1937 and (EU) 2020/1828 (Digital Markets Regulation).

ISO and UNI Technical Standards

ISO 31000:2018 - *Risk Management*: Guidelines for implementing risk management, applicable to assess risks in technological products and artificial intelligence.

ISO 27001:2013 - *Information Security Techniques*: Information security management systems, critical for cybersecurity and personal data protection.

ISO/IEC 27005:2018 - *Information Security Risk Management*:

Guidelines for managing risks in information security and data protection.

ISO/IEC 38500:2015 - *Corporate IT Governance*: Guidelines for the governance of information technologies within organizations.

ISO/TS 15066:2016 - *Collaborative Robots*: Technical specification for the safe design and use of collaborative robots, relevant for workplace safety involving human-machine interaction.

ISO 10218-1:2011 and ISO 10218-2:2011 - *Safety Requirements for Industrial Robots*: ISO standards defining safety requirements for the use of industrial robots in automated systems.

UNI EN 818 - *Series of standards regarding lifting chains*: Safety requirements and technical specifications for lifting chains, vital for ensuring safety in logistics and heavy load lifting.

UNI EN 12385 - *Steel Wire Ropes*: Safety requirements for the use of ropes in lifting systems, including design, construction, and testing to ensure product integrity.

ISO 13849-1:2015 - *Safety of Machinery - Safety-Related Parts of Control Systems*: Guidelines to ensure that machinery, including connected and automated devices, has safe control systems.

UNI EN ISO 14120:2015 - *Guards - General Requirements for Design and Construction*: UNI standards for the safe design of machinery and guards for operator protection.

ISO 14971:2019 - *Medical Devices - Risk Management Application to Medical Devices*: Essential for the safety of technologically advanced medical products.

ISO 45001:2018 - *Occupational Health and Safety Management Systems*: Guidelines for managing worker safety in industrial contexts, relevant for new technologies and automation.

ISO 37301:2021 - *Compliance Management Systems*:

Requirements with guidance for use, vital for ensuring product compliance and supply chain integrity.

THE AUTHORS

Carmelo Greco is a professional journalist. He currently leads the online publication Elzevir.it, an experimental project combining artificial intelligence and editorial expertise to pioneer a new form of cultural journalism. In the past, he has contributed to various outlets, focusing on economics, culture, society, and issues related to the nonprofit sector. In recent years, he has specialized in exploring the new frontiers of digital transformation, analyzing the impact of technological changes on business models and organizational processes. He has written several plays performed at the Siracusa Penitentiary, three of which were included in the collection *L'Italia e altre commedie* (Edizioni di Pagina, 2016). He is also the author of the novels *Le stagioni di Cavabella* (Libromania, 2016), *Focara di Sangue* (Fogliodivia, 2020), and *La strada di Miriam* (Scatole Parlanti, 2023), as well as business case studies *Sui banchi del Salento* (Rubbettino, 2019) and *L'innovazione fatta bellezza* (Rubbettino, 2024).

Roberto Sammarchi is an attorney based in Bologna, authorized to practice before higher courts and specializing in information law, digital communication, and data protection. He provides legal services in Germany as a European lawyer registered with the Munich Bar Association. He holds a PhD in legal informatics and IT law. He has also earned a master's degree in tax law and completed advanced training in administration, finance and control, food law, and EU law. Since 2007, he has been a lecturer in the master's program in clinical engineering and medical devices at the University of Bologna, teaching a course on legal responsibilities in technical and healthcare professions. An innovation manager and internal auditor, he is actively involved in several associations, including AIAS (Italian Association for Environment and Safety) and Federmanager. He is the author of numerous publications on digital technology law, and in this series on Enterprises and Rights, he has authored *The New German Supply Chain Act (Lieferkettengesetz): A Practical Guide with Italian Translation of the Law and Due Diligence Procedure* (2023) and *The Rights of the Ocean: A Guide to Understanding the UN High Seas Agreement* (2024).

www.ingramcontent.com/pod-product-compliance
Lightning Source LLC
Chambersburg PA
CBHW070954240526
45469CB00016B/880